First World War
and Army of Occupation
War Diary
France, Belgium and Germany

59 DIVISION
176 Infantry Brigade
174 Machine Gun Company
23 February 1917 - 28 February 1918

WO95/3021/13

The Naval & Military Press Ltd
www.nmarchive.com
Published in association with The National Archives

Published by

The Naval & Military Press Ltd

Unit 10 Ridgewood Industrial Park,

Uckfield, East Sussex,

TN22 5QE England

Tel: +44 (0) 1825 749494

www.naval-military-press.com

www.nmarchive.com

This diary has been reprinted in facsimile from the original. Any imperfections are inevitably reproduced and the quality may fall short of modern type and cartographic standards.

© Crown Copyright
Images reproduced by permission of The National Archives, London, England, 2015.

Contents

Document type	Place/Title	Date From	Date To
Heading	WO95/3021/13		
Heading	59th Division 176th Infy Bde 174th Machine Gun Coy Feb 1917-Feb 1918		
Operation(al) Order(s)	Operation Order No. I By Major R.G.S. Eyre Commanding 26th Bn. Royal Welsh Fus		
Heading	War Diary of 174th Machine Gun Company From 23/2/17 To 29/3/17 Vol I & II		
War Diary	Grantham	23/02/1917	23/02/1917
War Diary	Southampton	24/02/1917	25/02/1917
War Diary	Havre	26/02/1917	27/02/1917
War Diary	Longeau	28/02/1917	28/02/1917
War Diary	Warfusee	01/03/1917	01/03/1917
War Diary	Abancourt	02/03/1917	06/03/1917
War Diary	Foucaucourt	06/03/1917	08/03/1917
War Diary	Berny	09/03/1917	20/03/1917
War Diary	Fresnes	21/03/1917	22/03/1917
War Diary	Misery	22/03/1917	26/03/1917
War Diary	Brie	27/03/1917	30/03/1917
Heading	War Diary of 174th Machine Gun Company From 31st March 1917 To April 29th 1917 Vol 3		
War Diary	Brie	31/03/1917	03/04/1917
War Diary	Estrees-En-Chaussee	04/04/1917	05/04/1917
War Diary	Bernes	06/04/1917	09/04/1917
War Diary	Flechin	10/04/1917	11/04/1917
War Diary	Montigny Farm	12/04/1917	14/04/1917
War Diary	Jeancourt	14/04/1917	28/04/1917
War Diary	Bernes	29/04/1917	29/04/1917
Map	Map		
Heading	War Diary of 174th Machine Gun Company From 30th April 1917 To 31st May 1917 Vol 4		
War Diary	Bernes	30/04/1917	07/05/1917
War Diary	Roisel	07/05/1917	23/05/1917
War Diary	Bouvincourt	24/05/1917	31/05/1917
Map	174 Machine Gun Coy		
Miscellaneous	Relief Orders By Capt L.C. Benins Comdg 174th Machine Gun Coy	21/05/1917	21/05/1917
War Diary	Equancourt	01/06/1917	12/06/1917
War Diary	Metz-En-Couture	12/06/1917	24/06/1917
War Diary	V 6a.9.3	25/06/1917	28/06/1917
Heading	War Diary of 174th Machine Gun Company From To Volume 6		
War Diary	Fins	01/07/1917	06/07/1917
War Diary	Barastre	07/07/1917	31/07/1917
Heading	War Diary of 174th Machine Gun Company From 1st Aug 1917 To 31st Aug 1917 Vol 7		
War Diary	Barastre	02/08/1917	23/08/1917
War Diary	Bouzincourt	24/08/1917	31/08/1917
Heading	War Diary of 174th Machine Gun Company From Sept 1st 1917 To Sept 30th 1917 Vol 8		
War Diary	Winnezeele	01/09/1917	18/09/1917

War Diary	Brandhoek	19/09/1917	20/09/1917
War Diary	Vlamertinghe	21/09/1917	23/09/1917
War Diary	E of Ypres Gravenstafel and Frezenberg Sheets 1.10.000	23/09/1917	30/09/1917
Miscellaneous	174 Machine Gun Company Action Of Our Own Troops	12/09/1917	12/09/1917
Map	K.3.		
Miscellaneous	Message Form		
Miscellaneous	Fire Organisation Orders	26/09/1917	26/09/1917
Miscellaneous	174 Machine Gun Company Report On Recent Operations E. Of Ypres 26-27 September 1917	27/09/1917	27/09/1917
Map	Gravenstafel		
Miscellaneous	M.S.C		
Heading	War Diary of 174th Machine Gun Company From 2nd Oct 1917 To 31st Oct 1917 Vol 9		
War Diary		02/10/1917	14/10/1917
War Diary	Lens Sector	15/10/1917	21/10/1917
War Diary	Carency	23/10/1917	31/10/1917
Heading	War Diary of 174th Machine Gun Company From 1st Nov 1917 To 30th Nov 1917 Vol 10		
War Diary	Carency	01/11/1917	07/11/1917
War Diary	Avion	08/11/1917	12/11/1917
War Diary	Avion Sector	13/11/1917	17/11/1917
War Diary	Carency	19/11/1917	19/11/1917
War Diary	Berneville	21/11/1917	21/11/1917
War Diary	Courcelles-Le-Comte	23/11/1917	23/11/1917
War Diary	Heudicourt	24/11/1917	27/11/1917
War Diary	Ribecourt	28/11/1917	29/11/1917
War Diary	Fontaine-Notre Dame Sector	30/11/1917	30/11/1917
Heading	War Diary of 174th Machine Gun Company From 1st Dec 1917 To 31st Dec 1917 Vol 11		
War Diary	Fontaine Notre Dame Sector	01/12/1917	09/12/1917
War Diary	Lechelle	08/12/1917	08/12/1917
War Diary	Flesquieres	10/12/1917	16/12/1917
War Diary	Ruyaulcourt	17/12/1917	20/12/1917
War Diary	Barastre	22/12/1917	31/12/1917
Heading	War Diary of 174th Machine Gun Company From 1st Jan 1918 To 31st Jan 1918 Vol 12		
War Diary	Berlencourt	01/01/1918	31/01/1918
Heading	War Diary of 174th Machine Gun Company From 1st Feby 1918 To 28th Feby 1918 Vol 13		
War Diary	Berlencourt	01/02/1918	08/02/1918
War Diary	Bienvillers	09/02/1918	09/02/1918
War Diary	Durrow Camp Morv	10/02/1918	11/02/1918
War Diary	Noreuil S.E of Bullecourt	12/02/1918	28/02/1918

Woods 3021/13

59TH DIVISION
176TH INFY BDE

174TH MACHINE GUN COY.
FEB 1917-FEB 1918

174 M.G. Coy

1918

SECRET

Appendix "II"

Operation Order No. I
by
Major R. le S. Eyre
Commanding 26th Bn Royal Welch Fusrs

25th Batt. King's Liverpool Regt. relieve left front and support Companies of 26th Bn Royal Welch Fusrs on the night of 29th/30th September.

17th Batt. Royal Sussex Regt. will relieve the right front and support Companies of 26th Bn. Royal Welch Fusrs on the night of 29th/30th September.

Guides will be at rendezvous of both Battalions at 8-15 p.m.

Lewis gun Limbers will be at LEVANTIE EAST POST M5a.19 at 8.45p.m Great care must be taken that all Petrol Tins be carried out and loaded on limbers.

Platoons will on completion of relief proceed by usual route and occupy billets as follows:—

"A" Coy. CARTERS POST

Original

Army Form C. 2118.

WAR DIARY
or
INTELLIGENCE SUMMARY

(Erase heading not required.)

Vol I.

Confidential

War Diary

of

174th Machine Gun Company.

From 23/2/17 To 29/3/17

WAR DIARY
or
INTELLIGENCE SUMMARY

(Erase heading not required.)

Army Form C. 2118.

Instructions regarding War Diaries and Intelligence Summaries are contained in F. S. Regs., Part II. and the Staff Manual respectively. Title Pages will be prepared in manuscript.

Place	Date	Hour	Summary of Events and Information	Remarks and references to Appendices
SOUTHAMPTON	23/2/17	9.30 P.M.	1/4" Unit. bn. entrain for SOUTHAMPTON	Nominal Roll of Officers
SOUTHAMPTON	24/2/17	6.10 A.M.	Detrained at SOUTHAMPTON QUAY. Regiment attached to 59th Division	Capt. BENNS
		3 P.M.	2/Lt PALMER & 25 O.Rs embarked on S.S. LONDONDERRY	Lt BIXTON R.K.
		4 P.M.	Remainder of regiment embarked on S.S. KANFAH	" NEWTON H.S.
		5 P.M.	Advanced party sailed	2/Lt PALMER M.N.
	25/2/17	11 A.M.	Sailed from SOUTHAMPTON	" DAY M.N.
		12 noon	Advanced party landed at HAVRE and proceeded to No 2 Rest Camp	" DODD A.N.
HAVRE	26/2/17	12 noon	Convoy landed at HAVRE and proceeded to No 2 Rest Camp	" BUCHENAN C.S.
	27/2/17	12.30 P.M.	Entrained to area of concentration with H.Q. 1/8" Leic" Bde	2/Lt WOOD C.G.
				" IREDALE H.M.
				" HOGATE J.D.
LONGEAU	28/2/17	7.30 P.M.	Detrained LONGEAU. Billeted at the 6 taught. Informed attached to 178 Inf. Bde	
SARFUSEE-ABANCOURT	1/3/17	10.30 am	Bn marched SARFUSEE-ABANCOURT, on arrival billeted there.	
	2/3/17	?	Billeted at SARFUSEE. Inter tramy. Route March.	
	3/3/17	?	Col. 6, O.SC Scott and 1 O.R proceed to BERNY to report to O.C. 176 M.S.	
	4/3/17	12 noon	Ex 6 reconnaissance preparatory to relief. On arrival Jun Scott and four Lewis gun teams	
			with from GT. of 6 HQ. 1/6 N.S. Gy. 2 O.Rs to Field Ambulance (Sick).	
			Details valence & Kitchen to BERNY.	
FOUCACOURT	5/3/17	?	Company marches to FOUCACOURT, H.Q to Co H.Q. 2/6 S. STAFFS detachment.	
	6/3/17		2/Lt H.C. HEANE and 29 O.Rs report for duty with 4 Lewis guns. H Co. 2/6 S. STAFFS and	
			from 1/5 NOTTS & DERBYS) 4 O.R 2/5 N. STAFFS report for duty as carrying part.	
			Company notified of attachment to 176 & 2nd Inf. Bde	

Army Form C. 2118.

WAR DIARY
or
INTELLIGENCE SUMMARY
(Erase heading not required.)

Instructions regarding War Diaries and Intelligence Summaries are contained in F.S. Regs., Part II. and the Staff Manual respectively. Title Pages will be prepared in manuscript.

Place	Date	Hour	Summary of Events and Information	Remarks and references to Appendices
FOUCAUCOURT	7/3/17	7 P.M.	N°1 & 2 Sebats leave for Hospital at BERNY to relieve Dove & Sebat 151 M.S.Cy	
		10.30 P.M.	2/Lt HEARNE & Lewis Guns teams relieve 1st Kahn Grp of 149 M.S. Cy. In enfilade trench BERNY	
	8/4/17	7 P.M.	N° 3 & 4 Sebats and Coy HQ leave for Hospital & relieve remainder of 151 M.S.Cy. Coy HQ taken over and established at T.3.a.1.2. (Ref. Ancre) Details Report FOUCAUCOURT — M.H.S. Naval, T.O. with Hospl, L.C.M.S., with Ambs. Q.M. Stn and G.O.Ts.	
BERNY	9/3/17		Enfilade 2 Sebats. 16 guns and 4 Lewis guns in front. 3 Stabs to Serret Wood. Trenches very bad condition, especially C.Ts. In front of 2nd Class.	
	10/3/17		Activity on GRENADIERS reserve line.	
	11/3/17		1 OR wounded, to Hospital. 2/Lt D.D. HOLSATE wounded (slightly) to Hospital. 1 OR wounded to Hospital. 30 gas shells fell near 2 M.S.S. in DONICLES trench	
	12/3/17		1 O.R. from Hospital. 1 O.T. to Hospital (sick) Stahl in hospl.	
	13/3/17		1 O.R. wounded 1 T.O.R. wounded shrapnel/strafe. 1 O.R. sick to Hospital. 1 O.R. wounded gas to Hospital.	
	14/3/17		1 O.R. died effects of gas poisoning. 2/Lt C.G. LORD wounded slightly to Hospital. 1 O.T. Sick to Hospital. Conference of Command Officers with Brig-Genl. 176 & 2 Bde. ref. reorganization of M.S.S. Plan in Sectn is arranged to withdraw 4 guns from front. to be used as a Sector En-masse in the Ecclesiastic Line.	
	15/3/17		Plan to above carried into effect. 3376. Pte DESFOSSES. Killed for handing 14 air night type G.S. Rifle Grenade related to 175 Anthoine. Notice of R.S.C. in Maintaining Cadre Army to Gas Shelling in recovery hospital. No shots down a day - a C.T. to the team to Rain steel, so strong wind for (1 German Report) Felix self	

WAR DIARY or INTELLIGENCE SUMMARY

Army Form C. 2118.

Place	Date	Hour	Summary of Events and Information	Remarks and references to Appendices
BERNY	16/3/17		2 hrs later. 1 O.R. Sick to Hospital.	
	17/3/17	6 A.M.	Enemy evacuation of the trenches observed. Patrols reported all clear. S. of SOMME. Infantry and cavalry FRESNES.	
		7 P.M.	2 N.C.O.s each of N° 1 & 2 Sections supplied Infantry on their line along MARCHELPOT – VILLERS-CARBONNEL road, E. of FRESNES – MAZANCOURT, and on the N. & S. of the Sub. Halte Stellung in valley between MISERY and on new front line. Shot from Somme received (picked up) 1 O.R. to Hospital, sick. 538588 W.Staff to Hospital, self-inflicted wound (accidental pistol) 4 O.R.s from 416 S. Staff attached as Sanitas.	
	18/3/17		Situation unchanged. No hostility / shelling or activity. Hostile aeroplane activity reconnoitring above our front line. 2/Lm. D.D. Holgate from Hospital to duty. 1 O.R. to Hospital, sick. 67105 C/E Tillman T.H. to Divisional Eng. Course.	
	19/3/17		178th Inf. Bde. Field Co. R.E. par changed to bridge SOMME canal at WEST SUBURB – ST. CHRIST. Cavalry pass ours into our lines in hostile trenches front lines E. of SOMME-CANAL. 3 O.R.s from 2/5 N. Staff attached as Sanitas	

WAR DIARY
or
INTELLIGENCE SUMMARY

(Erase heading not required.)

Army Form C. 2118.

Place	Date	Hour	Summary of Events and Information	Remarks and references to Appendices
BERNY -	20/3/17		Establishment. H.S.S. interchanged.	
FRESNES.	21/3/17		Lt. 9 O.C. No 3 & 4 Sections reconnoitre for 8 H.S. parties supplying 3/5 & 2/6 W. Staffs. during relief. POULE-VERTE Road Station T.24.a.5.2½ and T.12.d.10.9. (Ref. Trench map Sheet 62c.S.15.) (5.O.T.D.); also parties for 2/1 S.S. to replace the ST CHRIST Bridge Head & Boat Site party about U.8.C.9.9. W.20.a.5.6. (same Ref. map). Company H.Q. reconnoitred at T.17.a.3.8. (Ref. Sheet 62c S.11.) 2 O.T.C. R. Hospital, Site. 1 O.T.C. from Hospital. 4 Chafeurs transferred to 177. C.S. Coy.	
	22/3/17	11 A.M.	Lt. Cy & O.S.C. N° 1,3 & 4 Subs ride forward to reconnoitre POULE-VERTE Road, and for H.S. parties from W. SST-SUBURB to CIZANCOURT to command main bridge and footbridge on SOMME at ST CHRIST. Company H.Q. moved to T.17.a.3.8. Company accommodated in dug-outs in MAZANCOURT with one Section near Coy H.Q. 176 Infantry Bde H.Q. moved to CHATEAU MISERY. 1 O.T.C. evacuated and shade of/shape (Site).	
MISERY	5 P.M.		Transport and Q.M. Store moved from FOUCAUCOURT to BERNY. Orders received from Brigade to have ST CHRIST and the Bridge head with a Section of H.S.S. N of the river at all parties already reconnoitred.	
	23/3/17			

WAR DIARY or INTELLIGENCE SUMMARY

Army Form C. 2118.

Place	Date	Hour	Summary of Events and Information	Remarks and references to Appendices
MISERY	24/3/17		Coy H.Q. unchanged. No 1 Sect. to St CHRIST to erect the Bridge head. Constructed R.E. Emplacements at V.14.b.17, V.8.c.7½.9, V.2.c.4.6, V.2.a.6½.0 (Ref. Sheet 62 C.S.N. 1/20,000). In touch with 184 M.G.Coy on right — in CHAVECOURT and 175 M.S.Coy in ATHIES WOOD.	
	25/3/17		Transport and Q.M. Store moved up from BERNY to Coy H.Q. at MISERY. Corps reconnaissance of BRIE and ST CHRIST Bridge head at ST CHRIST.	6 N.C.Os to 2nd Army in reserve front
	26/3/17		Gun reconnaissance for Nos 2, 3, 4 Sections. Baths and cleanshape. 1st Sect — in ST CHRIST in-line m.g. emplacements. 20 ORs to Hospital (Scabies). 1 O.R. died in Hospital (Machine gunbulb).	
BRIE	27/3/17 9.30 A.M.		Coy Hqrs, Q.M. Store & Transport moved to 0.29.C.10.4½ near ATHIES WOOD (Ref. Sheet 62 C.S.15. 1/20,000). Coy HQ accommodated in stables with Coy H.Q. 12 M.S. Place in Brigade line (in rear). Creating BRIE Bridge-head line from 0.26.b.4.4. to U.3.a.7.2.9. No 1 Sect. in bivouac. 1 O.R. to Hospital. 176 M.G. coys in reserve from 27/3/17.	
	28/3/17		State done recommended — Coy will take this for officers of ¾ S.A.A. per M.G. and ½ S.A.A. per M.G. Instead Bole line. Co-operate arranged for. Exploit of limbers for more mobility in advance. 1st Sect. instructed. 2 ORs from Hospital.	
	29/3/17		S. Galion reshaped. Improvement of employments and sup N.E. accommodated.	

Army Form C. 2118.

WAR DIARY
or
INTELLIGENCE SUMMARY
(Erase heading not required.)

Instructions regarding War Diaries and Intelligence Summaries are contained in F. S. Regs., Part II. and the Staff Manual respectively. Title Pages will be prepared in manuscript.

Place	Date	Hour	Summary of Events and Information	Remarks and references to Appendices
BRIE.	29/30 Mar	12 M.N.	Strength as at 29/30 March 1917. Officers 10* O.Rs 170✝ *includes 2/Lt. C.G. WOOD] in Hospital 3 O.Rs [signature] Leslie Denny Captain C. in Coy 174 Machine Gun Company	

Army Form C. 2118.

WAR DIARY
~~INTELLIGENCE SUMMARY~~
(Erase heading not required.)

Vol 3

Confidential

War Diary
of
174th Machine Gun Company

From 31st March 1917
To April 29th 1917

Original

Place	Date	Hour	Summary of Events and Information	Remarks and references to Appendices

Army Form C. 2118.

174th Machine Gun Company

WAR DIARY
or
INTELLIGENCE SUMMARY
(Erase heading not required.)

Instructions regarding War Diaries and Intelligence Summaries are contained in F.S. Regs., Part II. and the Staff Manual respectively. Title Pages will be prepared in manuscript.

Place	Date	Hour	Summary of Events and Information	Remarks and references to Appendices
BRIE	31st Mar		Company still forming BRIE Bridge-head with 12 guns. Company H.Q. at D.29.c.10.5. (Ref. Sheet 62c.1:40000) Several still had influenza. Gradually getting better. Enlarged to state 10.R. Evacuated to C.C.S. attd. 1/5 Sheept. No of Bde in reserve.	
	1st April		F.G.C.H. held at by H.Q. upon 1 Sgt. Beatie, 1 Cpl Carlisle, Pte Smith and Brennan, all of 184 Coy to 1st A.S. "Drunkenness"	
	2nd April	2.15 P.M.	NEWTON hand injured. His arrival from Beaudevais. ETAPLES taken in sheept.	
	3rd –		1 OR. (driver) on strength on Base Depot.	
ESTREES-EN-CHAUSSEE	4th –	11 A.M.	Company moved ESTREES-EN-CHAUSSEE into billets. No guns in position. 1 OR. sick to hospital.	
	5th –		2 OR. sick transferred to hosp. 1/5 sheept. 3 OR. hospital sick. Return Normoy and return.	
BERNES	6th –	11 A.M.	Company moved to BERNES and billeted. With H.Q. arrangements and shelters from 175 M.S. Coy. Divisional line attacked with 3 Brigade Front. 176 Bde Bde in centre, Bde H.Q. at NOBESCOURT FARM. Ct. by hell 111th Infe. Machine Gun Advisory Officer Lt Col EVANS and 2nd Lt. 75.M.G. Coy.	
		12 noon	at 178 Bde H.Q. BERNES to consult and co-ordinate brigade attack by 178 & 176 Bde 10 at 61st Div (on their right) upon high ground S.E. of LE VERQUIER. Arranged for the Coy to cover N.W. and S.E. faces of LE VERQUIER with M.S. barrage and so cover the 178 Bde attack from hostile M.G. fire upon the plate. Coy H.Q. established at U.4.d.5.2.	

WAR DIARY
or
INTELLIGENCE SUMMARY
(Erase heading not required.)

Army Form C. 2118.

Instructions regarding War Diaries and Intelligence Summaries are contained in F.S. Regs., Part II. and the Staff Manual respectively. Title Pages will be prepared in manuscript.

Place	Date	Hour	Summary of Events and Information	Remarks and references to Appendices
BERNES.	6th April	3 P.M.	O.C. Cy and O.C. Subns reconnoitre frontiers to carry out this scheme. Parties fixed as follows:- 3 guns YR 2 Sectn on sunken road running S.W. from JEANCOURT from L.32.a.6.2 to L.32.c.2.7 (Ref Sheet 62c N.E. 1/20000) to cover N.W. face of LE VERGUIER. 3 guns of Nº 4 Sectn astride L.26.a.0.2. to cover S.W. face of LE VERGUIER.	
		9 P.M.	Orders received the rest of the parties. Nº 1 & 3 Sectns used as carriers.	
	7th	12 M.N.	Artillery barrage opened, all at H.S.S. opened fire. 1 E.R. Shrapnel S.26.	
		12.40.	178th Bde Stks Britsn attacked. 2/Lt. C.G. Wood to V.K. on 3 weeks sick leave (Croinders)	
		1.30.	Nº 4 Sectn guns ceased fire as at this time no barrage shells have reached head of C.T. running N.E. of LE VERGUIER at L.33.d.9.2.	
		5 A.M.	Nº 4 Sectn guns withdrawn as other parties would have made rifle fire from LE VERGUIER hopeless.	
		8 A.M.	Nº 2 Sectn withdrawn. Number of wounded fried 16. Infantry reported on fire fell well in the village almost of them. No casualties. attack unsuccessful.	
		NOON	[struck through] ... O.C. to Bdn H.Q., ordered to reconnoitre frontiers E of HESBECOURT to cover FERVAQUE FARM. So frontiers right flank of 177 Bde who attack COTE WOOD 2 + 3 (Ref Sheet 62 N.E. L.16.C) at 6.30 p.m.	
		2.30 P.M.	Frontiers reconnoitred by O.C. Cy 2/Lt PALMER & 2/Lt DODD as follows:- 2 guns at L.15.a.7.8. both guns one S.W. face of FARM + snapshot shooting Journal L.16.C.6.5. 2 guns at L.14.b.5.0. to fire along the road running E through the FARM and arms weeds alt L.a.a.9.0. 2 final L.20. a 9.3. to cover Germans who use N.W. face of the FARM.	

WAR DIARY or INTELLIGENCE SUMMARY

Army Form C. 2118.

Place	Date	Hour	Summary of Events and Information	Remarks and references to Appendices
BERNES.	7th Apl.		2/Lt J.T. CROCKER having reported for duty from 198th M.G.Coy, 174 Inf.Bde. taken on strength. 3 O.R.s Sick transfered to Div. Cyclists Rest Station.	
	8 "	10 A.M.	Conference Bn. Cos. & 176 Inf.Bde. at HERVILLY to discuss probable attack by the Bde. on night of 9/10th upon high ground N. of LEVERGUIER, between GRAND PRIEL WOODS and PIEVNEL WOODS. Artillery and M.G. barrage above took place & Bde. which was to form a wedge and turn about its flank turning S. to attack LEVERGUIER itself. Artillery firing all day on Bde. front all day. Enemy reported plane active from high ground N. of LEVERGUIER. 2 Enemy Battle Planes seen.	
	9 "	2 A.M. to 6 A.M.	2/Lt Dodd with 2 guns took positions L.16.c.6.5 and L.20.a.9.3. fired upon enemy wire for L.21.a.8.7 to L.21.d.7.0 to keep the gaps cut by artillery. Each gun fired 4,000. Enemy reported to have retired from LEVERGUIER.	
		3.30 P.M.	The attack N. of LEVERGUIER cancelled. Brigade order N°13 temporary Plans for M.G. barrage with 11 guns upon ground at L.22.a. GRANDPRIEL WOODS & neighbourhood in accordance with B.O.O. N°13 submitted to Bde. H.Q. below 2 objectives.	
		6 P.M.	2/Lt Dodd and 2 guns withdrawn.	
		9 P.M.	Orders received from Bde. to place two guns at L.15.a.7.8 and L.20.a.9.3. to cover FERVAQUE FARM, which had been evacuated by the enemy, but was reported to be attacked by him during the night. These guns to fire on S.O.S. Signal. 2/Lt T.T. CROCKER i/c p.	
			2/Lt N.L. PALMER to Hospital sick.	
FLECHIN.	10"	2 P.M.	In accordance with Brigade O.O. N°14 the Company relieved 175 M.G. Cy. at FLECHIN. Brasier and Neap billeted with a the surface front and 178 Inf.Bde. going into reserve at BERNES. H.Q. established at Q.17.a.2.1. and N°3 Section in Coy. reserve at Coy. H.Q.	

2449   Wt W14957/M90 750,000 1/16 J.B.C. & A. Forms/C.2118/12.

Army Form C. 2118.

WAR DIARY
or
INTELLIGENCE SUMMARY
(Erase heading not required.)

Instructions regarding War Diaries and Intelligence Summaries are contained in F. S. Regs., Part II. and the Staff Manual respectively. Title Pages will be prepared in manuscript.

Place	Date	Hour	Summary of Events and Information	Remarks and references to Appendices
FLECHIN.	10th April	4 P.M.	Nos 1 & 2 Sections in the line. 2/Lt Cooke's 2 guns (No 1 Sect) moved to L.27.b.3.10. He pushed reconnoitred posts by by 2/Lt GILSHENAN to kennel in front of an hospice on road from No 95 this L.28. and so protect posts from attack from GRAND PRIEL FARM and ASCENSION FARM from Field lightenery. 2/Lt Sketch with 2 guns (No 1 Sect) to LE VERGUIER to relieve 2 guns of 7th M.G. Coy at L.34.a.3.5. and L.34.a.7.4. The Coys GRAND PRIEL and ASCENSION FARMS respectively. 2/Lt Day with No 2 Sect retired after 2/25.4.5 & at R.9.a.9.6. R.3.a.10.5. R.2.b.7.4. R.2.b.10.3.	
		11 P.M. 8 P.M.	Tracing of 8 guns positions made out sent to Bde H.Q. for information this division. Order received for Bolt H.Q. to reconnitre and instruct posts for 16 guns for defense yet available this.—— Heavy shelling of LE VERGUIER all night. 2/10/11? 1 M. discharged from 111 Inf. Post Station taken to Etaples.	
	11th	2 P.M. to 7.15 P.M.	OC 145 reconnaissance of Bde front and positions chosen for 14 guns for defense plans. 2 guns mounted as anti-aircraft in FLECHIN. Heavy Shelling of LE VERGUIER. (defensively there on 2 M.S.s the Stables. Dung reconnaissance shelling in .... Shelling started R.3.a.5.6.	
		6 P.M.	Orders received for Bde H.Q. to move to MONTIGNY FARM where Bde H.Q. had moved this day. and for Transport & Q.M. Store known as BEERNES. 2/Lt NEWTON Sect to MONTIGNY FARM to reconnitre accomodate.	
		11 P.M.	Tracing & Heavy Shelling of LE VERGUIER. 6 guns No 2 Sect withdrawn from L.34.a.3.5 moved to L.27.b.2.8. During the Heavy Shelling of LE VERGUIER from L.34.a.3.5 moved to L.27.b.2.8. The Coys GRAND PRIEL FARM as before. 4 OR's on shift from Bde Post Station. 1 O.R. to hospital, wounded. 111 Coy's Post Station.	

WAR DIARY
or
INTELLIGENCE SUMMARY

(Erase heading not required.)

Army Form C. 2118.

Place	Date	Hour	Summary of Events and Information	Remarks and references to Appendices
MONTIGNY FARM	12th April	1 P.M.	Company H.Q. and some details moved to MONTIGNY FARM at K.35.d.5.D. by H.Q. men accommodated in shelters. 2 men prisoners moved to Corps H.Q.	
		2 P.M.	Transport and W.H. Stores moved to BERNES. O.C. by Telegh. H.Q. to see S.B.C. Before Scheme of Defence was approved by S.O. M.G. Bde Hqrs. O.C. of portable attack on night of 13/14 by the through GRAND PRIEL FARM and ASCENSION FARM. H.S. posted to the recommender to form a gap further than Koha and a Howitzer E of Hon. to present counter attack. Parties above as follows 2 guns = PIEUVEL WOODS. 2 guns in further ventolment R.S.C. exclu. (Ref. 62° S.E 1:20000) 1 O.C. wounded answered stm C.S. 1 O.C. developed todn't from C.O.S. on subject.	
	13th "	12 noon to 6.30 P.M.	Reconnaissance by O.C. and 2/Lt Kitchener for 2 M.S. positions in R.S.C. extent. found at 10°3 Part at R.S.a. 2.3. Attack laid out in afternoon found ASCENSION FARM unoccupied and present thereat but was fired to retire. Then closed to comp. headqtrs of SECOND PRIEL and ASCENSION FARMS in night of 13/14th and plans were advanced as under. Carefully 2/Lt Day with two guns one moved forward to R.S.a. 2.3. to barrage fm. 4. 32. C. 5. 4. along the road country N.E. Security the flanks attack for a counter-attack from on right flank. and 2/Lt Wheeler with 2 guns was moved forward to PIEUVEL WOODS to barrage in front of PATRATINS along the road running N.E. fm STEADY PRIEL FARM through G.24. and G.19.b.); and along the road running thru E. fm STEADY through G.3ea and G.25.L. Three guns in Ronton by FPM with rolles of bin. ony of use S.O.S. Signal station. 6 the sny nor top. Chi - two additional patrols of the S.O.S. Complete with Lewis Barrage Plans spread were from the Captn. Office.	
		8 P.M.	Returned to Ebble by was former 15 H.A. passed to JEANCOURT. [1 OR sick to Hospital.]	

2449 Wt. W14957/M90 750,000 1/16 J.B.C. & A. Forms/C.2118/12.

Army Form C. 2118.

WAR DIARY
or
INTELLIGENCE SUMMARY
(Erase heading not required.)

Instructions regarding War Diaries and Intelligence Summaries are contained in F. S. Regs., Part II. and the Staff Manual respectively. Title Pages will be prepared in manuscript.

Place	Date	Hour	Summary of Events and Information	Remarks and references to Appendices
MONTIGNY FARM	13th April	11 P.M.	S.O.S. 76th Bde rang up S.G. to confirm at Bde H.Q. & forward position to barrage with front of the FARMS, following the orders: 1st Gun at L.27.a.8.5. firing 83° to 91° Hof. Overhead elevation 670. 1st Gun at L.28.a.7.3. " 107° to 115° Hof. 6°41' 1st Gun at L.28.a.2.8. " 103° to 69° Hof. 4°27' 1st Gun at L.34.a.7.3. — Between SECOND PRIEL & 7°12' ASCENSION FARMS. 2 Guns at R.5.a.2.3. between G.32.c.2.1 & 5°5' ASCENSION FARM	Ref Sheet 62 N.E. and 62 B.N.W. and 62 S.E. 1:20,000
	14	12.45 AM 3 A.M.	Enemy fails to attack. SECOND PRIEL FARM occupied without opposition after a truce fight of 12 hours. Machine gunners firing clear leaving guns un-captured. Counter-attack driven off great enemy E. & W. through L.30 and L.25 drove M.G. nest to position.	ASCENSION FARM occupied
		8 A.M.	M.G. barrage support advanced further unopposed, reached the front & to effect one N.L. & S. looking Active patrols activity and alive teams & elevated set-up below.	
		10 A.M.	L.T Bordes and intel Park JEANCOURT to prepare & reconnoitre of enemy ASCENSION FARM shelled & held by the enemy. Enemy rifles in high ground E. of ASCENSION FARM.	
JEANCOURT		2 P.M.	Coy. HQ. and advance Sect moved to JEAN COURT. 6 H.Q. established at L.26.a.5.4. Working the day no example in the village. Shots fired in the ground. Enemy retired to M.E. N side of look to the valley running N.E. from JEANCOURT at about L.27.a.0.5. Heavy hostile counter-attack & the valley. Other company was subject ni. for 2 hour with H.E. No casualties	

WAR DIARY
or
INTELLIGENCE SUMMARY

Army Form C. 2118.

Place	Date	Hour	Summary of Events and Information	Remarks and references to Appendices
JEANCOURT	14 April	3 P.M.	Several SOS Sigs first daylight. 5th Shelly cross arg mt shelter n.e. of HUT. 2/L' D.D. HOLGATE to Hospital. Scaglio went at n.o. buried mine. 200 rounds of ammo pump willite thrown and moved to R.E. dump. No. 1 Platt. Armored Cars. Twenty yds of patrol of four enemy men were talken in Pele Pod w.r.e ate sub-sect to Rlc of I.mount of garrison. Anti-Tank guns posted at L.28.a.2.5. and L.28.c.1.5. Total Guns ready at L.29.a.8.6. and extra making N.N.E. and E from this.	
	15th	10 A.M.	2/L' P.M North to 2/L' Day as S.back Offr. was 2/L' Colgate to Hospital. Company informed the Shelters and made Shelter front. 2 guns of A 2/3 Section mounted for anti-aircraft fired in Shell place during stand-mg. — 2/L' Silchiram to guard his guns from DAY of aeroplanes and reconnaissance from G. Shells off attention from doing the morning.	
			2 Ors to Hospital (sick).	
	16th	1 P.M.	50-G.O.C. 76 I.Bde at Bn. H.Q. %6 N. Staff. Bn. and was informed of our 17 I.Bde on my left held this from VILLERET (captured during night of 15/16) to CHATEAU (L.23.a) 106" I.of. Bde were on right holding line 20/70 long (parallel to and L7.2.7. just west from N.I.L. called this TUMULUS (Rof Sheet 62 B.S.W. 1:20000). The Bde wearily found taken on main line of resistance from 17 will maintain air. As the the of our posts holding to the puncks. bn had found this between the Supporting line. Sky-lights the smoked out well in summer of this new position. This necessitated bringing up G.O.C. left - arrange for the ground bombard the St Helen Battus Suffolks L.G.O.C. left reconnoitred in valley E of LE VERQUIER at about	

Army Form C. 2118.

WAR DIARY
or
INTELLIGENCE SUMMARY

(Erase heading not required.)

Instructions regarding War Diaries and Intelligence Summaries are contained in F.S. Regs., Part II. and the Staff Manual respectively. Title Pages will be prepared in manuscript.

Place	Date	Hour	Summary of Events and Information	Remarks and references to Appendices
JEANCOURT	16th April		L.35.a.central	
		4 P.M. to 8 P.M.	Reconnaissance began by 2nd & 4th Lt Littleton for the positions. Posts formed as follows:— 2 guns at about L.35.a.2.0. } To Range about high ground on 120 Centre & get answers from 2 guns at about R.5.b.7.6. } about G.20.c. Central to ours ravine at G.33.a.32.9. Arrange for 4 guns supporting posts to the highest ground there. 1 O.R. sick evacuated to Field Amb Rest Station. 1 O.R. Sick evacuated to Hospital. 2 O.R.s from Hospital.	
17th			Situation unchanged. Took up emplacements and shelters for guns from as above. Teams working upon shelters at R.5.b.7.6. Shelled by enemy from Koudom G.31.d., 10.8. 1 O.R. sick to Hospital. 2 O.R.S sick evacuated to F.C.S. Two guns N° Section at positions L.27.a.8.5 and L.34.a.7.3. Moved forward to positions L.35.a.0.0 and L.35.c.2.8. To Range from Wood in G.32. Central to Coots in front of ASCENSION FARM between Range Points 73° and 105°. Temporary Shelters constructed at these positions by Teams concerned.	
18th			Signal Bee note by Brig Genl C.V. Humphries Congratulating the unit upon its work whilst he was about to relinquish.	
		11 A.M.	Orders were by Brig Genl Humphries and reports new Ranges disposition as above appeared.	
		8 P.M.	2/G Section Relief. 6th LR Sub relieved N° Sub-hole left sub section and N°3 Section N° 2 Section. N°s Section.	
			Triple Sub Section 4/LIEUTS remain, viz. N°3 Section. Lt Hamilton Shelley of H.Q. N.E. of JEANCOURT. LE VERGUIER received its ordinary attention.	

Army Form C. 2118.

WAR DIARY
or
INTELLIGENCE SUMMARY
(Erase heading not required.)

Place	Date	Hour	Summary of Events and Information	Remarks and references to Appendices
JEANCOURT	10th April	9 A.M.	Divisional Order No. G.58 and Brigade Order No. S/191 received making dispositions as follows:- Nos 1 & 2 in support, 9th Division. Orders from R.S.A. about sig. to General line of the Brown trench to Hill in L.34.c., thence by road E. of LE VERGUIER and PIEUSSE WOOD to top of Gunner road about L.22.a.74.et.N. Role of the Command advance to wire the hole front and flanks a certain local. Strong Posts to be established at R.S. emplacements to be established forward of this line so as to avoid enfilading the intermediate zone of SECOND PRIEL WOODS. The line of posts from HATTENCOURT to HUTTEMENUS the R.S.B. as an advanced line. Plans completed for the main attack, and if necessary to command a counter attack.	See Appendix 17 showing the 8 Battn will employ Brigade for Reserve, front and Defence of Hamilton of Resistance.
		11 A.M. to 5 P.M.	St. Corps reconnaissance. Other main line of resistance in accordance with above defended left subsector, night by No. 16 Section Btn. arranged for front at L.35.a.o.o. to flank E. of SECOND PRIEL WOODS, and one valley in front of main line of resistance from WOODS to SECOND PRIEL FARM. Similar L.35.c.2.8. to flank on main line of resistance then slightly covering Monthy (Ascension) spur through L.35.c. and R.S.b. also the German strong points along the 120 Cateau W of ASCENSION FARM and SECOND PRIEL FARM. Posts also reconnoitred at L.34.b.1.3 and L.28.a. L.28.a.9.2 (allotted to Bm at L.28.a.7.3) and L.28.b.1.1. The two later Parties to assist in control on left flank. The Parties named Trenches from ASCENSION FARM (see heavy appended A) Subs-Front Shelly made Tn Trenches L.35.c.2.8. L.28.a.7.3 and L.28.d.2.6. No. 1-72 Sect's battled and fine & clear changes. 2/Lt. CROTHER to transport to muster T.O.	
		3.30 P.M.	20ths Sch. H Divisional Rest Sh. Ps. B.O. 5/194 received, embodying the following orders:-	

Army Form C. 2118.

WAR DIARY
or
INTELLIGENCE SUMMARY

(Erase heading not required.)

Place	Date	Hour	Summary of Events and Information	Remarks and references to Appendices
TEACOURT	19th/20th	10 P.M.	"Z" Coy Scouts with two parties attacked Butchers Row in attempt to ascertain if held. So far, men in Welshes and upon the main line of resistance, which is the West wall. Coy. OC. 174 M.G.S. to reconnoitre positions of M.G.S. on forward line of resistance, and brief specially hand picked men on information of tanks and along E. side of the Southern Section of GRAND PRIEL WOOD. Nightwing time to be used - Photos taken at Battn. Hqrs P.M. 20th inst.	* Appendix A.
	20th	—	Three 8-pointer chose and failed off. Attacked early. This scheme of defence of German line of resistance not affecting the barrage provided by staff from Front. An attached Schedule to H.Q. 178 IF Bde and approved of by B.O.C.	
		11 A.M.	N° 192 Scots Rifles employed thus in clearing pillboxes and keep of the Tank.	
		3 P.M.	8 Coy. & Batt'd with Headqrs to see new O.C. Brig. General CURRIE. D.S.O. was appointed O/c 8 Coy. the Bde. Section communicated those N° 8 & 94 Sections on the line. A replacement conducted at L.28.a.9.2. So an alternate defensive posn. From at L.28.a.7.3. (See Army) Emplacement conducted at L.34.b.1.3. 16.R. Scotts Rifles Hospital.	
		10 P.M.	Alternate emplacements for guns at R.S.a.3.3. and R.S.a.6.1. Conducted at R.S.a.2.3 and R.S.a.6.7.	
	21st	10.30 AM to 5 P.M.	O.C. 6/y, reconnaissance formed of GRAND PRIEL FARM, sniper's, enemy activity. All pm. of N° 3 Section and 94. Good visual and found suitable locations within supports. Arranged with F/Lieut. Br. Command. of M.G's Sub Sect. of staff WOOD at G.31.d.10.8. that held some snipers and a H.S. - on his guns at R.S.a. the local. Tank obstacle with 106 M.S.C. on our right, the left gun at R.S.d.0.0. firing between 3°25° TRUE.	

2449 Wt. W14957/M90 750,000 1/16. J.B.C. &A. Forms/C.2118/12.

Army Form C. 2118.

WAR DIARY
or
INTELLIGENCE SUMMARY
(Erase heading not required.)

Instructions regarding War Diaries and Intelligence Summaries are contained in F. S. Regs., Part II. and the Staff Manual respectively. Title Pages will be prepared in manuscript.

Place	Date	Hour	Summary of Events and Information	Remarks and references to Appendices
JEANCOURT	21st April		Breaks with an front at K.35.c.2.8. in Gricourt thevalley between the two Eulen and the machine of resistance in the right Sub-Sector.	
		2 P.M.	Visited the N°4 Sector in the afternoon found no occurrence.	
		11 A.M.	2/L⁺ Narsten transferred to work with N°4 Section left Sub Sector.	
		12 noon	Epice of Knenof. named Ropse Sector.	
		8 P.M.	Today that L⁺ INZ.L.O. 915 men from Sector is reserve fires up KTN 4 Section found in shellhole and new emplacements. Splendid firing. Shells exploded for mortars L.34. b. 1. 3 and K. 28. b. 1. 1. Employment made for new guns at K. 28. b. 1. 1. Forward guns in copse at L. 35. a. 0.0. Wired in front and in flanks	
	22	11 A.M.	1 M⁺ reinforcement from Red Depot. 1⁺ Bn⁺ inspected today M/G O.M. Stores, and found every satisfactory.	
		12 M.N.	2 guns of N°Sector with 2/L⁺ Dread fired as arranged with L⁺ S.N. Staffs (9.p.m. night & back)	
		2.15 A.M.	Wood at S. 31. d. 1.2.8. reported Loolsh German Snipers and a M.S. Number of guns to fire	
			4000.; from attacked emplacement at R.4. b. 5. 6 and R.5. C. 6.8. Knowing the wood. By Shrahel the guns also Shrapel on enemy trail reported to run between the wood and the river at S.32. Seked.	
		3 A.M.	Strong Infantry patrol sent out, found wood also spilt enemy label withdrawn down the hill devised up to hold the wood to the present. The Infantry are very pleased with this from guns.	
		9 A.M.	One of our Haebahn Balloons between MONTIGNY FARM and JEANCOURT brought down by a German plane. The observer escaped is his paraclalli.	

WAR DIARY or INTELLIGENCE SUMMARY

Army Form C. 2118.

Place	Date	Hour	Summary of Events and Information	Remarks and references to Appendices
TEANCOURT	22 April	11 A.M.	Lt. ROGERS to Divisional Gas School.	
		11:30 to 2 P.M.	O.C. & O/C Coy. Dan reconnoitred left of SECOND PRIEL FARM for positions of M.G. parties. Visited O.C. 2/6 N. Staff. Regt. and got correct disposition of his advanced posts. The enemy found the heavy bombardment posts in NO GARDEN – L.24 a. + c.	
		3:30 P.M.	Church Parade Service near Bn. C./C. JEOFFLIN at By.H.Q. of No.1 & 2 Sections.	
		8 P.M.	2 Guns of M.G. Section in close positions at R.3.b. 0.5 and R.3.a. 9.5. moved to emplacement positions at L.34. b. 1.3 and L.25. b. 1.1, and attached to 2/4 Leic. for relief of posts. A Carrying Party of 1 N.C.O. & 25 men for same better assist in the move. 2 O.R.s evacuated to C.C.S. Sick malaria.	
	23 "		Reports of Bn. Reporting tour and gas attacks of Reserve Sector.	
		3 P.M.	O.C. Coy. & 2/Lt. Dan visit Six Guns in Lt. Subsector under O.C. N/4 Leic. By H.Q. receive C/Sergt. Bee Sgt. nearing 2/6 N. Staff Regt. in Lt. Subsector. Gas attack last night. High General in L.24.C and L.30.a. and established posts. O/C. N/4 Leic. informed and will arrange to co-operate with emergency of response. 2/Battn. successful repel established.	
	24 "	8 A.M. 11 A.M.	F.S.C.M. on NSPHS S.W. R. Pl. refused to life attack named (in 17th March). Sealed 4253 Report P.R. R2	
		1 P.M.	Visited G.O.C. 176 of Bde.	
		3 P.M.	O.C. 9 reconnaissance visited O.C. N/5 Leic. and O.C. 2/5 S. Staff. Regt. 2/Lt. Silv Leic. to arrange to co-operate and support in letting attack through or hand in G.31 Central. 2/Battn. successful posts established.	

WAR DIARY
or
INTELLIGENCE SUMMARY

(Erase heading not required.)

Army Form C. 2118.

Place	Date	Hour	Summary of Events and Information	Remarks and references to Appendices
SEAPCOURT	25 April	10 A.M.	O.C. appointed Town Commandant of TERTRYCOURT. Took over billets of troops occupying the line and arranged for sanitary measures to be taken in the area. Battn. took over received & relief of 2/16 & 2/17 Rifles & 2/18 Bn on 27th inst. This coy to be relieved by 177 M.S. Coy. on 28/29 inst. 2/Lt Gooch rejoined 2/1st Bucks Bn at Int. School	
	26th		2/Lt Dowell & 2 O.Rs to No.43 Course, M.G.S.C. Base Depot Camiers. M.T. Wagstaffe to 13 C.C.S. (Sick) 1 O.R. (Sick) to Br. Post Stn.	
		10 A.M.	O.C. 177 M.S.Coy came up to arrange details of relief. Took over from Lyon Coy a relief sector K.	
		3 P.M.	Received orders that Enemy attacked 2/78th Rifles (on our left) upon QUARRIES and GOLDSAGE FARM, by demonstration with two Coys from QR's upon BUISSON-GAULAINE FARM - Company into rifle demonstration by 2 & 6 N. Staffords upon same objective. 2 guns of No. 3 Section attacked the Lake used at Martens L.29.a.6.4. Enemy shewed fire to Target at see 1000s (3.55 P.M.) and fired till dawn. Number of rounds fired 4000.	
		4.30 P.M.	Sub. Commander of 177 M.S. Co. reported C.H.Q. and freedom taken the relieved. Details of relief arranged by Sub. Officers concerned.	
		3 P.M.	2nd Command & BERNES Kamp to scheme of billets 177 M.S.C. some of our details.	
			QRH. Stn. BOUVINCOURT. Bn. from Montgomery relief for 24 hrs.	
	28th	11 A.M.	Transfer OOR's Stn. moved BOUVINCOURT — Section unchanged. 2/R.B. H.Q. moved to VRAIGNES on relief by 177 & 2/A.O. & BERNES.	
BERNES	29th		Relief of 2/R.B. 177 M.S.Coy to Coylaw 2/Bn BERNES.	

174 H.S. Coy Appendix "A"

INDEX

- ↗ Indicates gun positions & cones of fire in main line of defence.
- ↖ Indicates gun positions & cones of fire for Barrage.
- ⊕ Indicates guns now actually in position.
- × Indicates proposed positions of cubich emplacements & shelters are under construction.

1. On the S.O.S. signal being sent from the forward line, the Barrage guns can't open fire on the S.O.S. lines.

2. If this line were forced to retire as detailed, the main line of defence guns would then come into Play.

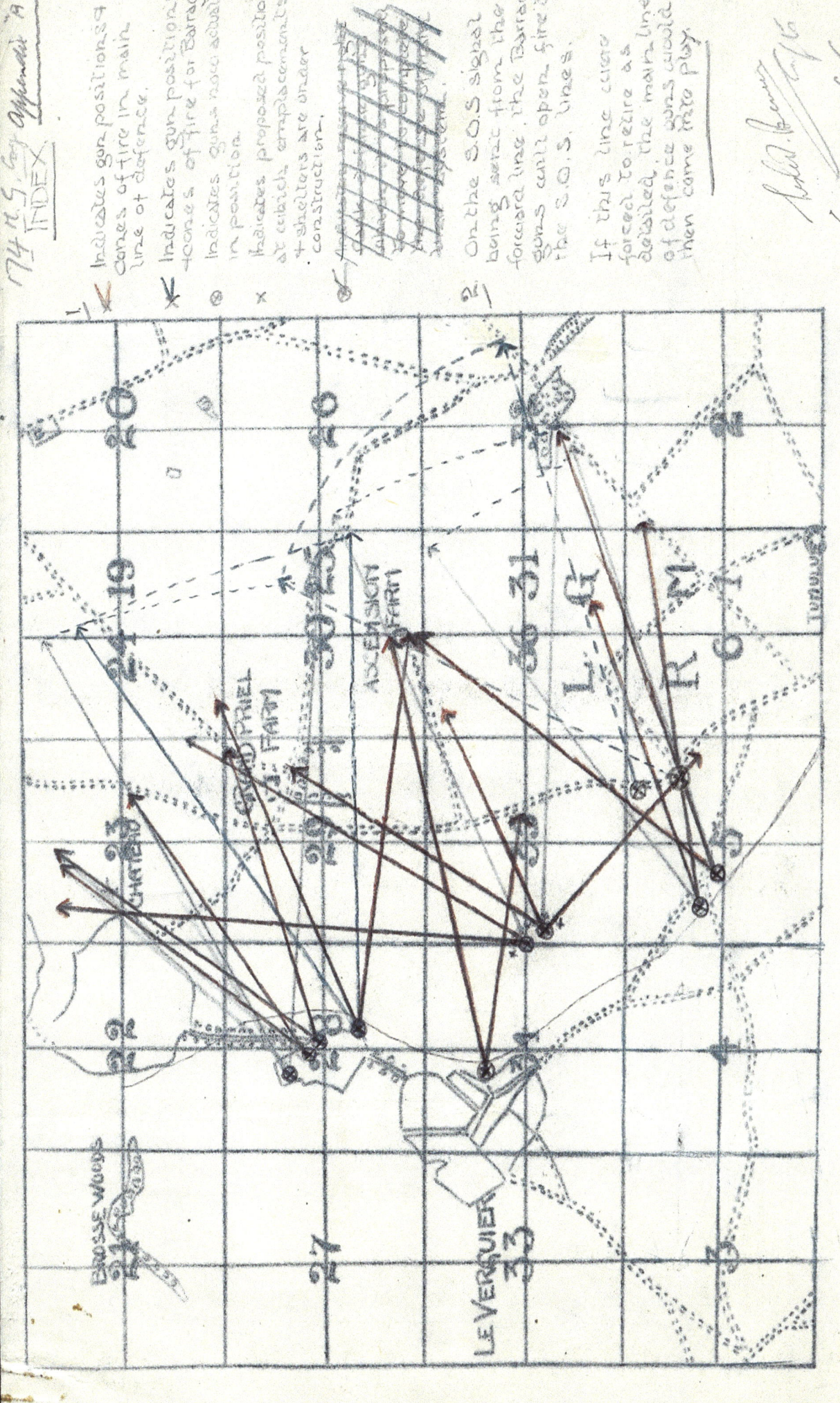

Army Form C. 2118.

WAR DIARY
or
INTELLIGENCE SUMMARY

(Erase heading not required.)

Vol 4

Confidential

Original

War Diary
of
174th Machine Gun Company

From :- 30th April, 1917
To :- 31st May, 1917

Army Form C. 2118.

WAR DIARY
or
INTELLIGENCE SUMMARY
(Erase heading not required.)

Place	Date	Hour	Summary of Events and Information	Remarks and references to Appendices
BERNES.	30th April		Company in rear billets at BERNES. Items Tomorrow, Bath, Rifles, Rifle & Bayonet. Clean up of Camp Area. 15 OR to Divisional Lan School for a course. Inspection to a Lecture by S.O.C. Rivalry of Flag Proof Latrine, and circuit lights. Football match against 1/4 K.O. Staffs Regt. drawn 1–1. 2 ORs to Divisional Rest Camp. 1 OR to Field Ambulance	
	1st May	10.15	Inspection of Company, Marshall was placed by S. O.C. 1/5/19 All Coys. who appeared satisfactory. Conform. Parade and Lecture by Sec. Commander on the General remarks of Discipline, Spirit in Infantry. 2/Lt E.G. Wood reported from Sick leave to O.R. 2 ORs reported arrived, 1 OR base Depot. 2 ORs sick, evacuated. 1 OR sick to Divisional Rest Ca.	
	2nd	9.30 12.30 2–3	Section training. One hour Drill. Physical Training. T.O.E.T. Elementary Drill, Lectures by S.O.S. on H.S.S. attack H.S.S. attack, Services on Artillery Scheme, Plot Report shot. 4 ORs sick to Hospital. 1 OR - D.R. Nurse. 1 OR on Draught from Corps Rest	
	4th	8.30 12.30 2–4	Section training continued. Attached NCOs exam (16 nobles) attacked from unit to whole released into to Battalion. 2 ORs sick to Hospital.	

2449 Wt. W14957/M90 750,000 1/16 J.B.C. & A. Forms/C.2118/12.

Place	Date	Hour	Summary of Events and Information	Remarks and references to Appendices
BERNES	5th May	10 AM to 2 PM	Section Training as above. Reconnaissance by O.C. of short fronts and M.G. emplacements in the RED LINE from HAMELET - BERNES - FLECHIN (the Divisional line) visited O.C. 75- M.G. Company at ROISEL reference relief ordered for nights of 7/8th May.	
		6 pm	Conference of commanding officers 176th Inf. Bde under G.O.C. at H.Q. 2/5 N. Staff. at HANCOURT reference impending Infantry offensive Scheme.	1 O.R. to Hospital (sick) 3 M.G. to Div. Rest Ctr (sick) 1 O.R. evacuated to C.C.S. (sick)
	6th	10 AM to 4 PM	On the R.G.C. Divisional Sector from 178 M.G. Coy at HQ 75 M.G. Coy at ROISEL to reconnoitre the line & visit O.C. and O.C. Sections visit arrange details of relief.	
		4 PM	Church Parade service at Company HQ.	
		10 PM	Infantry Bn. Relief 1/176 Inf. Bde relieve Inf. of 178 Inf. Bde in Left - Boce Sector. 176 Bde HQ opens at ROISEL.	
ROISEL	7th	11 AM	Transport & M.G. Stores move to ROISEL and take over HQ 175 M.G. Coy at K.16.d.4.2.4.	
		2 PM	Companies move to ROISEL and take over HQ 175th M.G. Coy as from 175 M.G. Coy at K.16.d.4.2.4. No. 1 Section, 2 gun teams and No.2 Section in reserve at HQ. No. 4 Section advanced near of TEMPLEUX.	
		11 PM	Relief completed. Disposal of guns of 174 Coy as follows:-	

WAR DIARY
or
INTELLIGENCE SUMMARY

(Erase heading not required.)

Army Form C. 2118.

Place	Date	Hour	Summary of Events and Information	Remarks and references to Appendices
ROISEL	1st May /18		4 guns in BROWN LINE, N of HARGICOURT (N° 2 Sect) 2 guns in VILLERET (N°1 Sect). 2 guns in trenches (in QUARRY) E of HARGICOURT (N°1 Sect). 2 guns mobile about in TEMPLEUX. See Trace of first cones & directives of guns. 8 Guns of 2nd M.G.C. (divisional) also Brigade Section under temporary Battalion disposal, as follows:- 4 guns in BROWN LINE, 2 guns S W of VILLERET, 2 guns mobile under in HERVILLY. See Appendix A.	See Appendix A
	2nd		2 guns M.G.C. reverted from am. Appendix supplementary	
			2 guns in N. SUNKEN ROAD fired 1500 rounds on gaps in enemy wire made by R.G.A. at F.30.C.4.1. and L.6.a.3.7. (Ref: Sheet 62 NE. F.2000)	
	3rd	10.30 am	Conference of C.Os with B.S.C. at H.Q. 32 N. Staff Offr of Bde Inspected attack by Battalion on NEW TRENCH in front of MALAKOFF FARM from trench M.N.O.F. with (ENFILADE) TRENCH vic. V.C. L.6.a.5.5. to gun of SWITCH TRENCH (R.f. Sheet 62 NE 1:20,000) Also splash attack in UNOPPOSED FARM (L.6.a.3.0) See Appendix A - Ready to form up in SUNKEN ROAD in front of SWITCH TRENCH on a two company front ready to attack at 9.30 (9.50 pm). Artillery programme arranged for a creeping barrage at 9.30 + to also standing barrage on objective. Latter consisted of battery at 9.30 + at 9.30 + to lift 100 - 250 yds beyond	Appendix A

WAR DIARY
or
INTELLIGENCE SUMMARY

(Erase heading not required.)

Army Form C. 2118.

Place	Date	Hour	Summary of Events and Information	Remarks and references to Appendices
ROEUX	3rd May	11 PM	The objective of the attack performed to UNNAMED FARM at 3.50 notably barrage on the FARM & left on the COLOGNE FARM (L.6.c.4.5) at 3.50 + H. Attack advance with objective at 3.50. Shaped of attacking infantry: — 2 companies to attack new trench 2 platoons to attack UNNAMED FARM. Machine Gun Programme arranged as follows. At 3.50 + 1 3 guns of 101 sect will 2/H Cheshire at L.5.a.7.8 to fire on UNNAMED FARM. to 3.50 + 4 S. At 3.50 + 4 3 guns in N. SUNKEN ROAD at about L.4.b.6.14 to barrage on the following to 3.50 + 85 objectives :— Shelter at F.30.c.6.8 MALAKOFF FARM ENFILADE TRENCH from L.6.a.9.8.5 to G.1.b.2.6 (Ref. Sheet 62ᵇ N.W) (1:10,000) SUGAR FACTORY At 3.50 + 8 3 guns in S. SUNKEN ROAD at about L.10.6.3.4. to barrage on At 3.50 + 43 gun at L.5.d.7.8. lifted on the COLOGNE FARM, so evening after Attack Establish attack that on the UNNAMED FARM and on the NEW TRENCH from Malakoff fire from the front. At 3.50 + 8 3 guns at N. SUNKEN ROAD to lift up on the following objectives — To several road running N.E. from Shaft two N.B.30.c.6.8 MALAKOFF FARM ENFILADE TRENCH, and also Rifle Pits at G.1.b.4.9.	

WAR DIARY
or
INTELLIGENCE SUMMARY

(Erase heading not required.)

Army Form C. 2118.

Place	Date	Hour	Summary of Events and Information	Remarks and references to Appendices
ROSEL	9 May	11 A.M.	Provisional fire plan held up in view of the objection brought up through accompanying R&R Colonel Sillabee.	
			Programme approved by F.O.C. and O.C. 750 Scotts for joint artillery.	
			Scouts & Seeks informed of this programme and necessary arrangements made.	
		2 P.M.	O.C. Bn. and O.C. 156 M.G. Co. met in loft at St Emilie and subject co-related. Arranged for B.Hm at 2.9.b.9.9. to take the 12" Scouts and barrage. Snd Recon made reconnoissance from Holmon's Bank and Reed Pits.	
		5 P.M.	Same. Synchronized and bn. set Bq. 20 H.S.G. 500	
		7 A.M.	Advanced Brigade Battle HQ. opened at RUELLES WOODS (L.7.c.9.5.)	
		8 P.M.	" " Bde at Gal HQ. DUNCEY (L.10.a.8.5)	
			Guards Confort.	
			7/17 ROD taken to attack in reserve.	
		9 P.M.	1 Section at SUNKEN ROAD fired 1000 rounds on Bofor w ranges near F.30. c.4.1. & 6.2.3.?	
		16 9.40 P.M.		
		9.50 P.M.	Zero line. Attack carried out in accordance with programme above.	
			Details as follows:-	
			Right attack got through the firstly for bit below where R.S. fire. Push the new frozen at 17.b.a.5. The left attack failed from strong M.G. & automatic rifle fire and was driven back by M.G. fire. The cut attack succeeded with a loss of three and about 15 men getting into the enemy trench due to Jet form. This party intracted consolidated and found little in mothbattes, capturing 3 small attack shelly some Jerring.	

WAR DIARY or INTELLIGENCE SUMMARY

Army Form C. 2118.

Place	Date	Hour	Summary of Events and Information	Remarks and references to Appendices
ROUSSY	8/9 May		NEW TRENCH was dug shortly held Defensive Defiladed was chiefly used by flank H.S. Bty - probably from high ground along NEW TRENCH S. of ENFILADE TRENCH unable to shell off Snarl on F.30.a. Artillery and H.S. programme was carried out without a hitch. Front attack replaced front of fire line on H.S. Bty which the essential the advance infantry was slowed into the core with the hollow slightly increased FARM. Lt Col THORNE Comg D.W.S. signalled partially taken out of boys gone late and confusion caused by M.S.S. intake. Roads from 4,500 yd farm.	
	9 May	5 AM		
	8 May	9.45 PM	A surprise attack was carried out by the 75th Staff Regt (single Staff Sub (a)) on ROUSSAY city from L.12.a.4.1. & L.g.7.6.3.4. Artillery and trench mortars started at 12.d.10.6. 2 guns of M.G. Sect under 2/Lt ?ensdale at L.12.c.1.7 and L.12.c.3.8. Fired 2,000 in support. Thro above from SCOTTO to C? 11.12 - in Supa Strade N.24 Cutof from L.6.C.S.S to S.1.d.1.2. The ?rate was firm in cover any bullets M.S. fire so enfilade riflemen at 11.30 PM carried by on H.S. Tre.	
	9"	6 AM 7 AM 11 AM 1 PM	O.C. refused B. gave HQ and gave husseen The escape danger O.C. ?band B9 HQ - ROSSEL O.C. ?sid before 200 H.S. Coy O.C. ?G Scotch in QUARRY, accompanied by 2/Lt Kilsham	
		11 PM	A patrol went out to exchange RAILWAY cutting and was covered by M.G. QUARRY at L.S.d. 10.10. The field field 500 rounds.	

WAR DIARY
or
INTELLIGENCE SUMMARY

Army Form C. 2118.

Place	Date	Hour	Summary of Events and Information	Remarks and references to Appendices
ROISEL	9/May	11 P.M.	Enemy S. at L.12, C.3.B. also fired 500 rounds in enemy trench N. of RAILWAY CUTTING N of the L.12	
			Owing to strong preventive storm (6 and 9th) for all sharp surveillance patrol work was sent out to post the N. of MALASSISE FARM. Gale stopped. Patrols were unable to approach the enemy wire.	
			OC 2ft. 150d Asks H.E. – QUARRY.	
	10	11 AM	OC 2ft. wife 3/Lt Gurkha from VILLERET – OC Tren Staff – to the – QUARRY (L.10.a)	
	10/11	1 PM	I consulted M.O.S. signalled from the HOSPITAL 2 from N. SUNKEN ROAD and	
		2 AM	1 Son in S SUNKEN ROAD fired 2000 per from on the sharing target.	
		11 AM	2/Lt Poole helped O2.75 to Staff Regt in relief from Rear trench L.H. at B.B.	
		2 PM	Consists of Krishmatts and fife Kunwars were but at the QUARRY (L.S.a) in vicinity of one fm. No casualties. { 1 OC – by strength from Brain Depot }	
		3 AM	{ 3 OCs – to hospital } { 1 OC (sick) – to hospital }	
	11	11 AM	S.O.C. IOC. Sec. were about BROWN LINE, wiring – one gun in rule	
		1 PM	Heavy Bombardment of QUARRY (L.S.a) by about 50 H.E. about 10 on H.Q. was from leave. No casualties.	
		2 PM	OC visited Sub.D.H.Q. and went up to 2/Lt Gurkha trench in QUARRY - L.S.a at 10.10. and at L.S.a 7.8 { 2 ORs (sick) to hospital }	
		9 PM	76 Lake Relief as follows:- { 1 – Dv. Corse Sc } { 1 – Cpl Restorts }	

2449 Wt. W14957/Mgo 750,000 1/16 J.B.C. & A. Forms/C.2118/12.

Army Form C. 2118.

WAR DIARY
or
INTELLIGENCE SUMMARY

(Erase heading not required.)

Instructions regarding War Diaries and Intelligence Summaries are contained in F. S. Regs., Part II. and the Staff Manual respectively. Title Pages will be prepared in manuscript.

Place	Date	Hour	Summary of Events and Information	Remarks and references to Appendices
ROISEL.	11/6/1.	10 P.M.	N°4 Section relieved N°1 Section in BROWN LINE	
		11 P.M.	N°3 Sect. 2 prs mer 2/15 P.H. N. Sect. relieved Z Coys post lent mer 2/15 Coote.	
		Midn'.	N°5 Sect. 2 prs. — 2/- Pickle in VILLERET (C.S. 200S)	
			(2 relief 2/15 Cooke who had been presented Brilote in TEMPLEUX)	
			Remain'd. 2/4 Sect N°2 Sect to VILLERET by H.Q. ROISEL	
	12th	9.30	O.C. N°4 Sect H.Q. Sect S.O.C.	
			S.O.C. informed Sect satisfact'y with sub section's in sights of H.Q. and watered at m'ble carried off attem'n. covered. Deposited grin infm'd and stand off' officer	
			S.O.C. form'd O.C.H. S'Coy S'Coolay During inspec'n probably the sections saturated later on went those as the march of S.O.C. to accident	
			implem'ts the shelter and contact excited BROWN and SECT line	
		11 A.M. to 2 P.M.	Reconnaissance of BROWN LINE hytnch and 2/L Coleman Assist'nt Compl'ment.	
			Spurs select'd at L.10.a.8.5. L.10.c.3.5. L.4.c.7.5. L.4.b.12. L.4.b.17	
			N. N. Ea. O.C. 3/5 S. Staff for R' Sub Sect and approach'd patches dress	
		6 P.M.	B.G.C. N' Sect G. H.Q. NE F Qualt'n of Staff' O/C — N°192 Sub/R bowles suf'f'd Gd.	
			O.C. N° Sect in B.G.C's meneys belts wealers. 2/L M. Shety	
			Reconn'ces conducted on L.10.a.8.5. L.10.c.3.5. L.4.b.c.7.5. 2/L M. Fwenston	
			Also the implem'nts conducted for Gorm. at L.5. at 10.10 and L.12.c.17	
			R.H. Point Lettice enlaced to apath'd a F./L Cor. ft Ho per Lan met easy turned	
	13"	11 A.M.	O.C. G goc arrive Ly Roe H.Q. here up H. hazle Quirrivyle	
			O.C. E. Jessies 2/15 Loods at Roe — VILLERET	
				1 O.R. evacuated to C.C.S.

WAR DIARY or INTELLIGENCE SUMMARY

Army Form C. 2118.

Place	Date	Hour	Summary of Events and Information	Remarks and references to Appendices
ROUSEL	13th May	3.45PM	Church Parade Service at Bac HQ. nr B W Staff Rgr nr Bac Chaplain	
	13/14		Aeroplane Enpleument evacuated at 1.4.6.7.12. Sent information 1600 yards front line at BOURLON ROAD. Up Mahamed form whom enemy was shelled the aeroplane earlier 8.12.13.	
	14"	1PM	Transit of firm & 11" Bde 136 C.G. on left (on his information) 2/Lt Day visited 12 H.S.G. and enhanced dispatch of ampons	
		6PM	B.C.Cr V Radcott Q. Sent S.O.E. and updated additional emplacement made & taken	
	15"	6AM	G.O.C. 169 Bde visited trenches. Well out seen from the contacy - Support of 2 VILLERET & VILLERET for South. Satisfied with everything. Visitant front line and moved around transtalle at 6.7.6.64 which appeared there no emplacement at "the Doup. No Gr 17" H.S.G. on our right, and Sent parties out (side of the flank from also visited from of 200 H.S.G. 1 O.R.(526) to Hospital	
	15/16		2 Teams report to Ordnance (L.S.G.)	
			We have 1 rifle report oders 1754 Feb - Brendrick 13th Bac. 5" Cavalry Divn. 13th H.S. Squadron	
	"27"9.6 Be men rifle returned by 13th Bde. 5" Cavalry Divn. 13th H.S. Squadron			
	Takes over taxes 12" H.S.G.			

War Diary / Intelligence Summary

Army Form C. 2118.

Place	Date	Hour	Summary of Events and Information	Remarks and references to Appendices
ROISEL	16 May	5 A.M.	O.C. 2/Hts. made visit 2/Lts Litstone and 2/Lts of VILLERET. Recommitted positions of S.E. Reams ? ? E of VILLERET. and have on journal photo at L.18.a.6.8. L.18.a.8.0. Patrol close in (sunset) L.17.a.6.8. Shelters E.T. Yser and Seman	
		6 A.M.	hides Monet. — N. of the men later removed by 5 Cavalry Division who relieve 57 Div HQ Visited C.H.Q. by E. Cap. H.S. asking they L.Cpl. Hough voices [?] Pte ? (IV Cap) Obn KatShoon returning (styled) out by IV Cavly Cps Rallied Cm. Off. (IV Cps out of this Cps) asked Sunders about Helic and dispatch (pre-SS) will arrived to contact Cavly Cps. H.S.Q. round the twin.	
		6 P.M.	O.C. To BRETEL S.O.E. Supplied parties for 24 ESS. Post at L.23.d.67. to one on photo, Per night L. ale.	
16/17			H.Q. Division in an information by 2 Cavalry Division 9/13 Boat holding half line confluence of SUNKEN ROAD Rent road vault of E from URIMMED FARM	
17		5 P.M.	O.C. G. visited 2/Ph.Posts from QUARRY and SLITTER TRENCH, and 2/Lts. Dughi and BROWN LINE	
		9 A.M.	Returned — Post at L.18.a.6.8 exhibits Many if am made of Cavly Cps H.S.O.	
		3 P.M.	O.C. G. 2/Hts. Day visits 13 H.S. Squadron on our right flange to see what and if our right flank took stands. From post at about start to ask belly L.24 a exit.	1 OR, evacuated to C.C.S.

2449 Wt. W14957/M90 750,000 1/16 J.B.C. & A. Forms/C.2118/12.

WAR DIARY
INTELLIGENCE SUMMARY

Army Form C. 2118.

Place	Date	Hour	Summary of Events and Information	Remarks and references to Appendices
ROISEL	17th May /18	4:50AM to 11:20AM	Fired N.M. 2pdrs, one in N Sunken Road, one in S Sunken Road, & in Enfilade Trench E. and were very satisfactory. Shoots from MALAKOFF FARM for anti-tank purposes. Reports of enemy garrison, reports of enemy garrison. Numbers began to fire at 3.0 p.m. Some harassed left and right Temporary Forts at SUGAR FACTORY.	
		11:30PM to 2 AM	During the night enemy shelled QUARRY (L.10.a) intense near LEHAUCOURT and for less than ½ hour. Also artillery who fired upon 30 Rd RHQ in 80 Rd FHQ.	3/1 OR from Hospitals
	18th	10 PM	2/1st Bay N HQ 2/5 S. Staff Rgt HERVILLY a number of P.E.C.H	
		6 m	H.S.S in N SUNKEN ROAD replied in ENFILADE TRENCH and MALANDER FARM.	
	19/5	8:30 PM	6 m H.S.S in N. SUNKEN ROAD fired 1000 rounds at about one dawn on these objectives, to cover garrisons coming in and retiring from their front lists.	
		4 AM	SL75 replied with falling right in on ENFILADE TRENCH by an Infantry at the flank at L.6.a.0.5.	
	19th	5:30AM	O.C. 6.2 visited 2/1st Newton and H.G. Bn at L. Sta. 6.9. and passed with Lt. Col. at L.S.L. 7.t. to inspect and see the night. The site with the side as a battle employment. HGC BG.C. in Return Visited Blackwood L.A.0.5.	
	15/20	9:30AM	and had good view of L.6.a.1. also MALAKOFF FARM. Visited O.C. 13th M.G. Squadron in TEMPCOURT and Pearson G Sq. in Canterbury in Tanks mutually supporting. Lt.Col. Bell 2/1 Bay 2 Teams N2 Sects. relieved 2/15 Ventz & 2 teams N2 Sects.	

2449 Wt. W14957/M90 750,000 1/16 J.B.C. & A. Forms/C.2118/12.

Army Form C. 2118.

WAR DIARY
or
INTELLIGENCE SUMMARY

(Erase heading not required.)

Place	Date	Hour	Summary of Events and Information	Remarks and references to Appendices
ROSEL	19/9/20		L. Section Relief. (Ca. 62) 2/1st Cooke relieves 4 teams N°2 Section relieved 2/1st Stapleton and 1 team N°4 Section VILLERS. 2/1st Stapleton and N°4 Section to TEMPLEUX vice 2/1st Cooke to rear of ROSEL. 2/1st Easton to TEMPLEUX vice 2/1st Cooke. Relief complete 4 P.M. L.M.Gun No. 4, 5 & 7.1. completed as a false emplacement. S.O.S. in the left. Ream team commenced. Quiet night.	
	20th	11 A.M.	Visited Hqrs 8th Bgde & M.S. Squadron - in on left Examined for plants on chalactic billet inspected by O.C. Company. in GREEN LINE	
		12 noon		
		2 P.M.	Inspected Transport by O.C. Company E/OR to Hospital	
		6 P.M.	O.C. to visit O.C. M.S. Squadron in BROWN LINE now on left at VILLERS FAUCON. E/OR instructed from Headquarters.	
	20/9/20	8 P.M.	Enough Plate Confession - BROWN LINE.	
		10.20	8 men Pioneers, for addition 2/1st Nash. to Schefter "COTE WOODS" . the last team for Pioneers for 19.9/1.17.23. to M.S.S. in SUNKEN ROAD from 1500 yards and in S. SUNKEN ROAD Antonich 24/9/17.23.3 from 2000	
		11.50	On ENFILADE TRENCH, Railway left of TEMPLEUX FARM Rotation 24/9/24/5.44.	
		3.25 to 3.45 P.M.		
	21st	12 Mid-to 10 A.M.	Rec. TR. with that 2 rafter Junction on rafter Junction of M.S. Squadron on night 22/23 each Battalion be at South Division. Visited day at N° M.S. Squadron at advance Pinkroad relief number P22/23. With O.C. of Section HQ QUARRY (L.10.a) to examine advance the line also arrange relief.	
		to 3 P.M.		
			5 O.T.Cs. (2/Lts) allotted.	

WAR DIARY
or
INTELLIGENCE SUMMARY
(Erase heading not required.)

Army Form C. 2118.

Place	Date	Hour	Summary of Events and Information	Remarks and references to Appendices
ROISEL	21 May		Arrangements made for hourly 20 firm. The line will to N. side of EPPEVILLE. All employment sent out by 200 M.S.G. based on a later employment also the party at L.S.d.6.8. as above one at L.S.6.7. The acting party to HULBERT. BROWN LINE awaited Central enforcement held E & S S.SUNKEN ROAD L.4.c.7.5. N & N.SUNKEN ROAD L.4.6.1.2. L.4.c.1.6. N.SUNKEN ROAD 26	See Appx 4 "3"
		2.30PM	Arranged for travelling Officer and 1 OR. to proceed to spiritual Cy HQ ROISEL in 2 RH 2H for attachment to this fortification prepare take for 9 NCOs also left details for higher 22/23rd Assault Kearny Jul. leave " him likely on 23/24th Norfolk busted at Bipon Battle and shortly sharfort.	
		6PM	Relief was shown up and evacuated Tale Gnrl. Post. Trails Gunn + BEETON return from No.42 M.F. Ambulance Connaulg. Pte Rogers received fully shift by the COYS commander and war trip had by F.C.M.	
	21/22		New employment in N. SUNKEN ROAD contested at L.4.b.6.1.b. Additional Shelter provided for war later employment of relieving N.S. Squadrons	
	22	10AM	2/Lt Sitzbeson & No. 25 N Staff Regt. HERVILLY as member of R.E.G.C.M.	
		12 noon	Orders received for more of white company to BOUVINCOURT on 23rd at 3PM. 1st BURTON and NEWTON to BOUVINCOURT tomorrow billets accommodate.	
			2 OHS & 26 rgnts ft CS 1 OR - H div R & SA	

Army Form C. 2118.

WAR DIARY
or
INTELLIGENCE SUMMARY
(Erase heading not required.)

Instructions regarding War Diaries and Intelligence Summaries are contained in F. S. Regs., Part II. and the Staff Manual respectively. Title Pages will be prepared in manuscript.

Place	Date	Hour	Summary of Events and Information	Remarks and references to Appendices
ROISEL	22/23		Relief of this Company by 10th and 11th Machine Gun Squadrons, 4th Cavalry Division in accordance with instructions already issued and detail noted above.	
	23"	4.10am	Relieved Section to billets at (B) HQ – ROISEL. Relief Completed.	
		Noon	Monthly report upon Tactical and Technical Lessons learnt during the month rendered to Bgde HQ.	
		1 P.M.	Transport and Q.M. store moved to BOUVINCOURT. 4 ORs on strength from Base Depot. 1 OR (Sig) to Hospital.	
		5 P.M.	2/Lts SILSHENAN and FREDDIE and 8 ORs to HERVILLY to meet 2" and 15" Lancers to guide them to QUARRY (K.3 central) and to stop at ROISEL in order to stay in support billets. Three similar parties of with these units ordered to shortly man this for [?] billets. 2/Lt WELSH + 20 men to billets BOUVINCOURT as advance party.	
BOUVINCOURT	24"	7.30 AM	176" Bde. HQ. moves to BOUVINCOURT.	
		11 AM	174 Machine Gun Company moves to BOUVINCOURT. Company HQ established P.7.a.7.0. – Billets previously arranged in town [?].	
	25"	9 AM	Company moves from ROISEL to BOUVINCOURT, cleaning of guns & general examination of Billets taken in. 12.30 PM 1 OR evacuated. 1 OR Sick to Hospital.	

Army Form C. 2118.

WAR DIARY
or
INTELLIGENCE SUMMARY

(Erase heading not required.)

Instructions regarding War Diaries and Intelligence Summaries are contained in F. S. Regs., Part II. and the Staff Manual respectively. Title Pages will be prepared in manuscript.

Place	Date	Hour	Summary of Events and Information	Remarks and references to Appendices
BOUVINCOURT	26th May	7-7.45	Physical Drill Parade incl. Colby Offrs.	
		9 to 12.30	Company Parade. Drill and Sections by Sections	
		6 P.M.	Company play Bn. H.Q. at football – drawn 4-4.	
		9 P.M.	Company Concert in Divl. Concert Party Hut.	
	27th	11.45 A.M.	Church Parade for non-conformists.	
		5.30	C of E	
		7 P.M.	Inter Section Football	
	28th	7-7.45	Physical Drill.	
		9 to 12.30	Company Parade as above. Brig. Genl. Currie watched company drill.	
		2 to 6 3.30	Rifle & Lewis Gun NCOs to Drill	
		7 P.M.	Inter Section Football	
	29th	7-7.45	Physical Drill.	
		9 to 12.30	Company Parade as above.	2 O.Rs. (sick) to Hospital
		10 P.M.	L/Cpl Burton, Naston and Ingate reconnoitre road to HAZECOURT-LES-BAS. The reconnaissance party under 2/Lt Bode in honor of Bn. move to Divisional area EQUANCOURT on 31st May 31st

2449 Wt. W14957/Mgo 750,000 1/16 J.B.C. & A. Forms/C.2118/12.

Army Form C. 2118.

WAR DIARY
or
INTELLIGENCE SUMMARY
(Erase heading not required.)

Place	Date	Hour	Summary of Events and Information	Remarks and references to Appendices
BOUVINCOURT	30 May	7.45 7.0 12.30	Megarial drill Company parade. Platoon training I.G. Lect. Football	
	31st		Infantry Battalions and H.Q. 174th Inf. Bge. have come to BOUVINCOURT as Divisional Reserve — Dinner (Lunch) Company still in same billets in BOUVINCOURT. Strength of Company Officers: Capt BEANS L.C. — O.C. Lt BURTON R.W. 2i/c NEWTON H.S. T.O. 4 Lt DAY H.H. HOOD C.J. DODD A.M. (in comd. of CARRIERS) 2/Lts IREDALE S. GIFFORD T.S. HOLYOKE D.D. (Hospital) NEWTON P.H. CRUISE R.F. Other Ranks — 171	

O.C. 174 M.G. Coy.

R.L.S. Beans Capt.

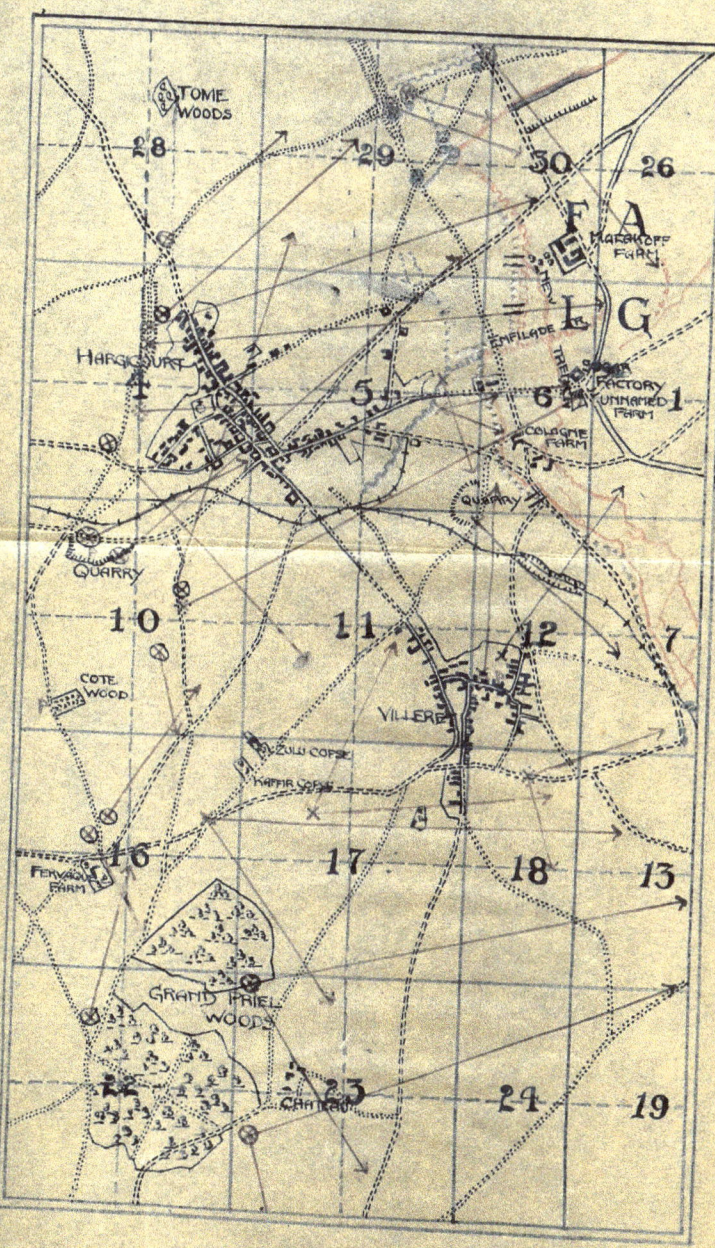

Relief Orders. Copy Appendix B
by
Capt L.C. Bennazi Comdg 174 Machine Gun Coy.

[Stamp: ORDERLY 21 MAY 1917 174 M.G. COMPANY]

21/5/17.

Relief On the night of the 22/23. May. the guns of this Company in the Brigade Sector will be relieved by guns of 10th & 11th Machine Gun Squadrons.

2. Additional Positions In addition to the existing positions of guns of this company the following positions will be handed over to incoming Squadrons as Battle emplacements.

A COTE. WOODS. GROUP:- 2nd Lt. Newton 4 positions in the BROWN LINE at L.22.a.7.5 L.16.a.7.2. L.16.a.8.4 L.10.D.2.7.

B Old positions at L.5.D.6.8 as well as new emplacements at L.5.B.7.1

C. Three existing positions at VILLERET all to be occupied

D. BROWN LINE positions 2nd Lt Wood additional emplacements in S. SUNKEN ROAD. Position in Cruciform Post L.4.c.7.5 Position in Trench E of N. SUNKEN ROAD at L.4.B.1.2. an additional emplacement in N. SUNKEN ROAD. at L.4.B.1.6.

3. Reserve Guns. 4 guns of the relieving Squadrons will be accommodated in Billets = TEMPLEUX. 2nd Lt Crocker will supply a guide to be at Cross Road L.2.D.6.2 by old Dug-outs at 8.30 pm to shew billets to incoming teams.

4. Guides Guides from all gun positions to be occupied will be at Section H.Q.:- Quarry at L.10.a. at 9.pm to guide in relieving teams.

5. Attachment The following personnel of relieving Squadrons will report at Section H.Q. QUARRY at 3 Pm. tomorrow 22nd for instructions prior to the Relief
4 Officers
1 O.R per Gun Team coming in

Relief Orders Continued   Sheet. No 2

6. The following details will be left behind in the Trenches for the night of 22/23 to be attached to 10th & 11th Squadrons.

    2nd Lt Newtons Group   2 N.C.Os.
    2nd Lt Woods   "   Sgt Mackintosh & 2 N.C.Os.
    2nd Lt Days   "   2 N.C.Os.
    2nd Lt Crockers   "   2 N.C.Os.

These N.C.Os are to be able to give all information about the positions occupied by their Groups, fields of fire, Range Cards, positions of Flank guns, German Trenches, our Trenches. They will remain with relieving teams until their services are no longer required, minimum time 24 hours. Rations for these N.C.Os will be sent en bloc to Section H.Q. tomorrow night.

7. Transport The following transport will be available at Section H.Q. at 10 Pm.

    2 Pack mules for VILLERET.
    2 Pack mules for 2nd Lt Days 2 Guns.
    1 Limber to COAT, WOODS and for No 3 Sections Guns in BROWN LINE

8. Hand Over The following will be handed over on relief and receipts given & received Copies to be sent to Coy H.Q.

    S.A.A.
    Belt Boxes
    Bombs.
    Very Lights
    Picks & Shovels (Trench only)
    Fly Proof Latrines
    Food Cup-boards.
    Gas Gongs.
    Sand Bags (less 2 carried per man)
    Weather Cocks.
    Range Cards.
    Creosol.

Relief Orders Continued   Sheet 3.

(i) Tripods will not be handed over.

(ii) 14 Belt Boxes of M.G. Squadrons are being dumped at Coy H.Q. where they can be drawn by Sections on Relief.

(iii) Instructions regarding Petrol Tins will be issued later.

IV Section Commanders will personally see that all Stores handed over especially Belt Boxes are in good Order.

9. During the relief Box Respirators will be worn in the alert position.

10. <u>Rest Billets</u>. On completion of relief Sections will proceed to Coy H.Q. ROISEL. where they will be shewn their Billets.

11. <u>Relief Completion</u> will be notified by Priority wire from LEFT Bn H.Q. by code word "WHISKY".

12. <u>Intelligence</u>. Range Cards will be provided and handed over for each gun position to be occupied. Section and Gun Commanders are responsible for handing over all information regarding their guns, positions, and fields of fire. This is especially necessary as the relieving Squadrons have had little opportunity of reconnaissance and are not habitually in Trenches.

13. <u>Maps</u>. All sketch maps, tracings and special Orders of intelligence are to be handed over and receipts obtained. Copies to be forwarded to Coy H.Q.

14. <u>Acknowledge</u>

Issued at 8 p.m.   8 copies

Distribution
Copy 1 to O.C. No 2 Section
 " 2 " O.C. No 3 Section
 " 3 " 2nd Lt Crocker
 " 4 " 2nd Lt Newton
 " 5 " T.O.
 " 6 " 176 Brigade H.Q.
 " 7 " War Diary
 " 8 " Spare Copy

_____ Capt.
O.C. 174 M.G. Coy.

ORDERLY ROOM
Date 21 MAY 1917
No........
174 M.G. COMPANY

174 M.G. Coy.
59th Division

WAR DIARY
or
INTELLIGENCE SUMMARY

Army Form C. 2118.
(Erase heading not required.)

Place	Date	Hour	Summary of Events and Information	Remarks and references to Appendices
EQUANCOURT	June 1st	2 P.M.	Company moved to EQUANCOURT to HELL Camp at V.16.6.2.3. (Ref. Sheet 57c S.E. 1:20000) 116th Inf. Bde Projects. 2/Lt A.V. DODD rejoined company from 42 Machine Gun Course COUILLES. 2/Lt K.T. BEATON having reported his arrival from Base Depot & 1 OR unfit for general duties reposted from Base Depot & 1 OR (sick) to Hospital.	
	2nd		Company in Billets cleaning and refitting. Sgt PARKER went to M.S. Company as C.Q.M.S. 1 OR to 41 C.C.S. with mental depression.	
	3rd	9.30	Brigade Church Parade.	
		2 P.M.	Brigade Sports. Company won Sgts Race, Officers race and 4 from Mile 12, three seconds and a fourth. Medical Officer visited Sanatorium.	
	4th	8 A.M.	O.C. 2/i/c Commander 2/Lts DAY, CUSHEADAN went to BAILLY. 2/Lt DALY & 2 Officers from 2/Lak Bns 176 Bde to visit TANK TRAINING GROUND — The afternoon and co-operation with this tank up to Same.	
		10 P.M.	G.O.C 176 Inf Bde visited the Camp.	
	4-15 P.M.	X.B.S.	Section Training. P.T. dine notes and arm drill, F.C.E.T. etc.	

WAR DIARY
or
INTELLIGENCE SUMMARY

(Erase heading not required.)

Army Form C. 2118.

Place	Date	Hour	Summary of Events and Information	Remarks and references to Appendices
EQUANCOURT	4th June	3 P.M.	Completion of Brigade Sports (in'C' Company Football championship, won by this Coy.)	
			1 O.R. Sick report.	
			1 O.R. reported in as stayed from 17 M.G.Cy	
	5 June	7-7.45	Physical Training	
		9-12.30	Section Training, Hun and arm drill. Mechanism, I.A. at	
		2-3	Section & S.O.S. — Wheel and extended fire	
		8.30	Company of Commanders Officers 176 Bde at Bde HQ to discuss training. Camp Duties and Sanitation and Inspired Transport Sports on 9 June.	
			Escorts sent to Bear Depot Copières as witnesses	
	6th	7-7.45	Company Training as above.	
		9-3	1 O.R. on sick report from Bear Depot.	
			2 O.R.s from hospital.	
	7th	7-7.45	Company Training	
		9-3	1 O.R. sick at Rftp.	
			1 O.R. evacuated to C.C.S.	
			1 O.R. " 111 Coys. Roster.	
	8th		Company Training as above, with athletic practice. Rifle exer. from hospital.	
			2 O.R.s Sick Rftp. 1 O.R. from Hospital.	

WAR DIARY or INTELLIGENCE SUMMARY

Army Form C. 2118.

Instructions regarding War Diaries and Intelligence Summaries are contained in F. S. Regs., Part II. and the Staff Manual respectively. Title Pages will be prepared in manuscript.

(Erase heading not required.)

Place	Date	Hour	Summary of Events and Information	Remarks and references to Appendices
EQUANCOURT	June 9-12"		Company training.	
		2 PM	Bayonet, Horse Show and Transport Sports. This Company won 3 firsts, and 1 second. Remarkable to the Company of "cooks" from kitchens, one brother from each section, sent one from the section thought the best winning Section. Firing by No1 Section, time 60 secs, from time Section began to move until firing in action.	
			2 OR's M Divisional Signalling Course.	
			1 OR. F.A. Hosp.	
	10"	9.30	Brigade Church Parade.	
		3 P.M.	50 OR's inoculated with T.A.B.	
		6.10	Conference of Commanding Officers. 9-76 Bde at Brigade HQ. regards relief of 176th B/Bde in A/r Sector (BILHEM) Divisional front on night of 11/12". This Company to relieve 175 Machine Gun Company on night of 10/11" to BURTON. relief 175 M.G. Coy H.Q. – METZ-EN-COUTURE (manuscript details of relief). Kt NEWTON relief T.O. MsH.S.G. at VALLU & ARTT WOOD (P.33.a)	
		2.30	OC "2/Lt. DOY & Lt. SHERIDAN at a lecture at Brig HQ by C.R.A. 59th Division upon Lt. & Artillery co-operation.	

2449 Wt. W14957/M90 750,000 1/16 J.B.C. & A. Forms/C.2118/12.

Army Form C. 2118.

WAR DIARY
or
INTELLIGENCE SUMMARY
(Erase heading not required.)

Instructions regarding War Diaries and Intelligence Summaries are contained in F. S. Regs., Part II. and the Staff Manual respectively. Title Pages will be prepared in manuscript.

Place	Date	Hour	Summary of Events and Information	Remarks and references to Appendices
EQUANCOURT	11 June	9.30	O.C. q OSC Nos 1, 2, 4 Sections & 175 Machine Gun Co. HQ. to METZ for a recce for reconnaissance of the line. Details of relief fixed up whilst officers received.	
		9-10.30.	All our guns fired in the 100" M.S. Coy at EQUANCOURT. First car transport spent in multiple cuttings moving	
	11/12 12 June	11 AM	Infantry fire the relief. Office 175 M.S. Coy to BUHEN Section. Rele HQ Staged at NEVILLE (P2, d5.8) Transport and H.M. Blue move to VALLULAR WOOD to relieve 175 M.S. Company at P.7.d.9.4.	
METZ-EN-COUTURE		3 P.M.	Company HQ moves to METZ-EN-COUTURE and takes over from 175 M.S. Company HQ at Q.20.a.3.3.	
		5 P.M.	O.C. 16th Brigade HQ. Orders received for O.C. to recce in a still-concealed handsaddle of RIBECOURT by the remarkable firm strongers the Coys on right of 13th. Guns 7.10 to 5.10 +2 mins. This company to arrange for frost of machine gun fire be opened on the HINDENBURG front line from Jas. +15 to Jas. +8½ mins. on the front from the road in K.36.d a. or L.31.c. inclusive to the road in K.35.a inclusive. Zero hour at 10 P.M.	
	12/13		Relief of 175 M.S. Co. by this company completed at 12.30 P.M. Disposition of guns in the Brigade Sector asked taking, see appendix A	

Army Form C. 2118.

WAR DIARY
or
INTELLIGENCE SUMMARY
(Erase heading not required.)

Instructions regarding War Diaries and Intelligence Summaries are contained in F.S. Regs., Part II. and the Staff Manual respectively. Title Pages will be prepared in manuscript.

Place	Date	Hour	Summary of Events and Information	Remarks and references to Appendices
METZ-EN-COUTURE	12/3		No1 Sectn with 1 Sec 9th 3 Sectn attacked in right Sub-sector. No 4th. No 2 Sectn in the 2 Emedia le line left	
			No 3 Sectn in company reserve at Empland Pte.	
	13th	10AM to 4PM	Good work fired during night on road running thro' K.36.a.42.31.c from M.S. at Q.11.b.6.6.4. O.C. Coy and "BURTON" visited Sectns 4 & 5 sectns and made now OP where Brigade feels. All guns of 4 Sectns in left Sub sector in action — O.C. 36 in staff in left Sub Sectn visited and inspected 4 M.S.S. explained. Also inspected plans to sheet Pts HINDENBURG LINE proposed to stop night Enfall known established. Similarly arranged with OC 36 W Staff Pagin right Sub-Sectn	OC reinforcement from A.M.T.D. From Bou Depôt 5 ORs
		5.20	Maent 5pm, as per attendees to Lieut-to Bdgde H.Q. O.C. to visited H.Q. with Plans for nights sheaf, and to Syn chronise time Plans approved by O.C. — as follows: Gun Positions. Objectives (Ref. Sheet 57.C.N.E. 57.S.E. + HINDENBURG LINE RIBECOURT sheet)	
			Q 5.d.0.1. Head of C.T. at K.35.b.64.	
			Q 11.l. 5.5.7. " K.36.a.1.3.	
			Q 12.a 13.4.2 " K.36.a.2.7.	
			Q 12.a 13.4.1 " K.36.a.6.6.	

Army Form C. 2118.

WAR DIARY
or
INTELLIGENCE SUMMARY
(Erase heading not required.)

Instructions regarding War Diaries and Intelligence Summaries are contained in F. S. Regs., Part II. and the Staff Manual respectively. Title Pages will be prepared in manuscript.

Place	Date	Hour	Summary of Events and Information	Remarks and references to Appendices
METZ-EN-COUTURE	16 Jan		Q.10.d.3.1. Q.11.c.1.3. } To traverse inwards along HINDENBURG front line from the wood Q.11.a.2.6. Q.11.d.6.4. } R.36.a. exclusive to the road in R.36.a. inclusive. To traverse along HINDENBURG front line from road R.36.a. inclusive to road R.36.c. inclusive. R.36.c. inclusive to road in R.36.a. and R.36.c. inclusive.	
		6.30	Bn. Commander on the line. Inspected the plans. Inspected trench saps Q.5.c. No. 1 & 2, See list, and flew & saw trench system and situated.	
		10.15 10.65	M.S. bombardment on HINDENBURG front line carried out in accordance with above plans. Number of rounds fired 5260.	
	13/14		3 Sects. fired during the night on the road running through K.26.d. and Q.3l.c. On no points at Q.11.d.64. 10 m.s. working war. Tunneling company on east of N.S. trench did dug out in Q.5.c. and Q.12.a. Note of improvement of bombers, Sentrels, outposts & M.Gs. sniper stations and Snipers posts continued.	
	14"	3 P.M. 7 P.M.	O.C. 2 Bgy visited O.C. My Sect. at his firm & right of R Sector. Visited at lest HQ. Bgy Corps. Machine Gun officer.	

WAR DIARY
or
INTELLIGENCE SUMMARY

(Erase heading not required.)

Army Form C. 2118.

Place	Date	Hour	Summary of Events and Information	Remarks and references to Appendices
METZ-EN-COUTURE.	14/15 June	During the night	During the night 1500 rounds were fired on the road running thro K.36. central and 480 rounds on road running through K.36.d. and L.31.c. Hostile M.G.s were active all night. An enemy patrol approx 5/6 attacked working parties on R.E. Tunnelled dg-outs & on front line (Lewis guns & trench battle) of machine gun turning.	
	15"	9 P.M.	"H" Day 15 "D" Bde R.F.A. "C" Batty fire a H.S. bombardment at "18" Visited all M.G. Lewis guns in the 2 Reserve line	
		6 P.M.		
	15/16		During the night 2000 rounds were fired on the road through K.36. central. Hostile M.G.s fair. Enemy machine gun at reference BEAUCAMP.	
	16.	10.15 P.M.	Visited Divisional Machine Gun Officer B.M. & O.C. Lewis guns.	
		11.30 P.M.	H.S. barrages put in R.H.Q.? Visited No 14 Lewis Guns - Front line and left of R.Batn H.Q. (Bed. Staffs)	
		4 P.M.	front line patrolled back area of HINDENBURG line obtained.	
	16/17		During the night 6" M.G.s fired 1480 rounds on the road running through K.36. central and through K.36.a. and L.31.c. Standing Line of enemy turf a period of about ½ hrs ride Barrage fire at 200 yds a front of an enemy front line between the Forward Support line and Reserve front line, the Forward Support Line.	

Army Form C. 2118.

WAR DIARY
or
INTELLIGENCE SUMMARY
(Erase heading not required.)

Instructions regarding War Diaries and Intelligence Summaries are contained in F. S. Regs., Part II. and the Staff Manual respectively. Title Pages will be prepared in manuscript.

Place	Date	Hour	Summary of Events and Information	Remarks and references to Appendices
METZ-EN-COUTURE	16/17 June		Sgt. Tunnecliffe was in Forward Support line, and no experience of enemy was at all they entered.	
	17.	9.30	Lt. McBee H.Q. referred report to Lt. None brighter down the on R.A.	
			line – 15" mg. ammunition required.	
		11.A.M.	By 16 or 2/1 Bde R.F.A. arrange to co-operate M.S.S and to relay	
			transpn. Cpl Col to Div Gas Course	
		12 noon	To Off. i/c Machine Gun Company men right to arrange for flak co-ordn.	
		3 P.M.	To B.C. 126 Machine Gun Company men on left. Arrange R. flank co-ordn.	
	17/8.		2/Lt. Day from attached to 2/1 Bde R.F.A. to assist Captain i/c for exp.	
			2/Lt. Seeler relieves N°2 Section at trenches.	
			Line N°3 Trench line formed Q.11.b. 6.5. with gun and relief 0.20 from 8003	
			Sections attached to N° Section, making up place at Q.11.d. 5.2.	
	18		Capt. BENNS. to U.K. on 10 days leave.	
	19.	9 A.M.	4 men and 1 N.C.O. attached to R.E. for Tunnelling Course.	
			O.C. visited OC N° 4, 1 and 3 Sections and went round whole Brigade Sector all guns with the exception of two intermediate line guns were visited.	
	19/20.		Building of new Transport lines and Q.M. stores at V.6.a.9.5. commenced. 2/Lt Iredale detailed to superintend the work. 0.20 4 rounds fired 11/16 J.B.C. & A. Forms/C.2118/12. Retalet in Road K.35 – K.29 from gun position at Q.11.d.6.4.	

Army Form C. 2118.

WAR DIARY
or
INTELLIGENCE SUMMARY

(Erase heading not required.)

Instructions regarding War Diaries and Intelligence Summaries are contained in F. S. Regs., Part II. and the Staff Manual respectively. Title Pages will be prepared in manuscript.

Place	Date	Hour	Summary of Events and Information	Remarks and references to Appendices
METZ-EN-COUTURE	20th June	9 A.M.	O.C. visited O's C No 4 and 1 Sections and went round the of Front line guns	
		5 P.M.	New front line joined up; O.C. visited 2/1 Bde R.F.A. a Machine gun and Artillery Barrage to hold good for the present.	
	20/21.		1000 rounds fired during night on Road K. 35 - K.29.	
	21.	2 P.M.	O.C. visited O.C. 200th Coy to arrange particulars of relief. 2/1st Div visited Intelligence Officer of Brigade giving him the exact positions of guns and their line of fire. During the day the building of 9 M.S. tres. erection of large wire structure at K.29.c.85.75. and have been for hostile standby was continued. Gunners were observed putting up large wire structure at K.29.c.85.75. Two guns using Centraid Sightt fired 2000 rounds on this road during the night. 240 rounds were also fired on Road K.36.680.	
	21/22.			
	22.	3 P.M.	Visited at C.H.Q. by Divisional M.G.O.	
		5 P.M.	O.C. and O.C. 200th Coy visited whole of Brigade Front also front line gun positions and 2 support positions	
	22/23.		1980 rounds fired on K.29.c.85.75.	
	23.		Coy relieved by 200 M.G. Coy during the day. On completion of relief Coy proceeded to new camp at V.6.a.9.3. Two teams for anti-aircraft at NURLU and YTRES.	
	24.	9 A.M.	Improvement of camp; latrines dug, grease trap made.	

Army Form C. 2118.

WAR DIARY
or
INTELLIGENCE SUMMARY

(Erase heading not required.)

Place	Date	Hour	Summary of Events and Information	Remarks and references to Appendices
V6 a 9.3.	25.	7.15 AM	Physical Drill.	
		9 A.M.	Section Officers kit inspection	
		10-12.	Interior Economy.	
			O.C. visited O.C. 2ro Machine Gun Coy at METZ.	I.O.R. to PERONNE on sanitary course.
	26.	7.15 AM	Physical Training	
		9 A.M.-12 noon	Inspection by Lecture Officer. Laying out of kit and improvement of Camp generally. O.C. visited anti-aircraft position at YPRES	
		3 p.m.	G.O.C.'s inspection of camp.	
	27.		Training. O.C. visited anti aircraft positions.	
	28.		Route march and Baths.	
		2 p.m.	2/Lt Day visited anti aircraft gun at NURLU.	

Lt. Burton 1st Lieut.
174 M.G. Coy.

Army Form C. 2118.

WAR DIARY
or
INTELLIGENCE SUMMARY

(Erase heading not required.)

Vol 6

Confidential

Original

War Diary
of
114th Machine Gun Company

From:
To:

Army Form C. 2118.

174 "Machine Gun Company"

WAR DIARY
or
INTELLIGENCE SUMMARY

(Erase heading not required.)

57 Division

Place	Date	Hour	Summary of Events and Information	Remarks and references to Appendices
FINS	July 1st		Company in reserve as Divisional Company at V.6.A.2.2.0. (refsheet 57c) Nr FINS. 176 Inf Bde with Coy relieved by 177 Inf Bde, on relief this company return to Bde Company. CAPT BENNS returned off leave U.K. 1st Lt. Sub Geoff. 1st Lt. rejoined from Sanitary School PERONNE. 1st Lt Sheffield wounded to C.C.S.	
	2nd	9-12.30	Section Training.	
		11 AM	O.C. & 2 Lt BURTON visit 2/Lt NOOD and 2 A.A. Guns at YTRES	
		6 P.M.	2nd Day of Conference of C.OS at Bde H.Q. relief by 57th Division reliefs by 58th Division of Bde and Division to BARASTRE 1st Lt Sub Lieuts Cpls E&SR 1st Sheffield to C.C.S.	
	3rd	9-12.30	Section Training	
		10.40	O.C. & 2 Lt BURTON visit 2/Lt DODD and his 2 A.A. Guns at NURLU.	
		6 P.M.	Visit by Cpls E&SR 1st Sub Sheffield to C.C.S.	
	4th	7-7.30 9-12.30	Section Training	
	5th	7-7.30 9-12.30	Section Training 1st Lt Sub 16th Cpls E&SR	
	6th	7-7.30 9-12.30 9 AM	Section Training O.C. & confirmation of C.OS at Bde H.Q. of move of the Bde to Camp C9 BARASTRE on 7th inst. and programme of Training for division who carried out during the Divisional Rest.	
		10.30	All C.OS proceed to BARASTRE via car to see new camps and the training areas.	

WAR DIARY or INTELLIGENCE SUMMARY

Army Form C. 2118.

Place	Date	Hour	Summary of Events and Information	Remarks and references to Appendices
FINS.	6 July	11 A.M.	2/Lt DAY & 12 O.Rs to next camp at D.Q. BARASTRE as advance party & prepare camp. 5 ORs return from sick list. 25th Tunnelling Company R.E. 2/Lt TEDMAN generally assists. LoRs 1st Div. Sigs. 1 OR from hospital.	
BARASTRE "7".	7"	5 A.M.	Company moved to Camp D.Q. BARASTRE. Coy H.Q. O.P.Q.R.S. (Ref Sheet 57c). 2/Lt B. DODD, BEATON and 16 ORs from A.A. work NURLU return to Company at BARASTRE. 1 OR to Hosp. 1 OR sick to Hosp. 176 I.O.Bde H.Q. and Battalions move Hoslopfe B.T.C.S. Hoslopfe C.9. Company on working parties to camp. 1 OR sick to hosp.	
	8"	9 A.M.	O.C. to conference J.T.O.s at the H.Q. reference camp discipline and training programmes for the ensuing week. Discussed w.Co. J sel times starting a stop for working parties to camp. Company employed on working parties in camp. 1 OR sick to Hosp.	
	9"	6.45-7:30 / 9-12:30 / 2-3:30	Company and section training.	
	10"	12 noon	176 Light T.M.B. arrive and are accommodated in the Company camp. 1 OR sick to 76th Staf. RACSR. Company section training as above.	
	11"		Ditto. 2/Lt WOOD. adsfg by 40" Division. 2/Lt. WOOD to hospital. 2/Lt WOOD and his two teams from YPRES rejoin company on C/C BEATIE to Div. Gas School. 10 R to V.R. on 16 days leave. 3 ORs sick to shipp to C.C.S.	

WAR DIARY
INTELLIGENCE SUMMARY

Army Form C. 2118.

Place	Date	Hour	Summary of Events and Information	Remarks and references to Appendices
BARASTRE	20th July		Company on 30 yds Revolver Range.	
			L/Cpl SUTHERS 1st Bn Sgd School 2/Lt J.T. CROOKER 1st Bn days Course with R.F.C.	
			2/Lt R.S. BURTON & Pte SHALDERS to U.K. for 10 days leave.	
	21st		Divisional Sports. 2/Lt G.D. TWOMEY from 2/6 S. STAFFS REGT attached for instruction and report.	
			Ammn to Latrs R.F.C. Conference examinations for NCOs & Selected Junior Cos.	
	22nd		Church Parade	
	23rd		Brigade Field Day. Attack practice. No 3 or section co-operated in barrage fire evening St. attack.	
			Co Officers attended lecture by Col. KELLY on Counter-Battery work.	
	24th		Section Training. Lecture by officer on Co Officers of Bn and M.G.s in attack.	
	25th		Section Training.	
		6 P.M.	Lecture by Capt BENN'S to Officers & NCOs of 2/6 S. STAFFS REGT on Co-operation between	
			Infantry and M.G.s in Defence and Attack.	
	26th		Capt BENN'S and section officers made to 6th 26th TRAIN'S HOY to inspect	
			ground preparatory to Divisional Tactical Exercise on 27th. Lieut Sgt DAUGHTON proceeded to Divisional One School for in	
			course.	

Army Form C. 2118.

WAR DIARY or INTELLIGENCE SUMMARY

Army Form C. 2118.

(Erase heading not required.)

Instructions regarding War Diaries and Intelligence Summaries are contained in F. S. Regs, Part II. and the Staff Manual respectively. Title Pages will be prepared in manuscript.

Place	Date	Hour	Summary of Events and Information	Remarks and references to Appendices
BARASTRE	12 July	6.45-7.30 9-12.30 2-3.30	Section Training.	
	13"		2/Lt CROCKER and 3 Section Co. Shoots with 2/6 Bn. S. STAFFS REGT on Bn. in attack. 1 OR. P.B. to Base Depot.	
	14"	11 A.M.	Training as above. Parti S.M.E. Course fired on Range. 2/Lt Shelton of Camp by Maj. Gen. ROMER. S. OC. 59" Div. 5 ORs rejoin, taken on strength from Base Depot. 1 OR. from Hosp.	
		G.P.M.	Conference of C.O.s of Bns. Pte. of S. OC. in sector, and having not aroused in nextweek. 2/Lt W.J. BEATON to IV Corps 2f School for Course. Cpl LEDDY "	
	15"		Church Parades. 1 OR. Sick to C.C.S. Hospital.	
	16"	6.45-7.30 9-12.30 2-3.30	Company and Section Training. 2/Lt DODD visited Severe Battlefields in a day tour under G.S.O. 1st Brigade. 5 ORs. on Strength as reinforcements from Base Depot. 3ORs (Sick) to Hospital.	
	17"		Company on Range firing Platz S.M.E. Course. 2 ORs Sick to Hospital.	
	18"		Company on Range firing Platz S. OC.S. Course. 1 OR. to Hospital.	
	19"		Company on 30 yds Revolver Range, Parti Table D. 2 ORs from Hospital.	

Army Form C. 2118.

WAR DIARY
or
INTELLIGENCE SUMMARY.
(Erase heading not required.)

Instructions regarding War Diaries and Intelligence Summaries are contained in F. S. Regs., Part II. and the Staff Manual respectively. Title pages will be prepared in manuscript.

Place	Date	Hour	Summary of Events and Information	Remarks and references to Appendices
BARASTRE	27th July		Company took part in Divl Tactical Exercise and was under orders of Devl. M.G.O. for purpose of barrage.	
	28"		Capt. Reeve proceeded on No.6 Lewis Gun ct. at M.G. School Camiers until 21st August.	
			Lewisers under S.O.i No. 43/67 Sergt Cole Y. & Cpl. Bennett W. returned from 45.679 Course Camiers. 2/Lt Breckenridge W. joined Coy. from Base Depot. 2.O.R. to Hospital.	
	29"		Church Parades. 2.O.R. to Hospital. 2/Lt Twomey E.W. returned to his Batt.	
	30"		Section Parades.	
	31"		Bde. Tactical Exercise. 2 Sections Nos 1 & 2 took up positions for barrage. 3.O.R. to Hospital.	

[Stamp: ORDERLY ROOM 14 AUG 1917 No. 174 M.G. COMPANY]

R.W. Buxton T.
t/ O.C. 174 M.G. Coy.

Army Form C. 2118.

WAR DIARY
or
INTELLIGENCE SUMMARY
(Erase heading not required.)

Instructions regarding War Diaries and Intelligence Summaries are contained in F. S. Regs., Part II. and the Staff Manual respectively. Title Pages will be prepared in manuscript.

Place	Date	Hour	Summary of Events and Information	Remarks and references to Appendices
Original			War Diary of 174th Machine Gun Company From 1st Aug. 1917 To 31st Aug. 1917	Vol 7 Confidential

Army Form C. 2118.

WAR DIARY
or
INTELLIGENCE SUMMARY.
(Erase heading not required.)

Instructions regarding War Diaries and Intelligence Summaries are contained in F. S. Regs., Part II. and the Staff Manual respectively. Title pages will be prepared in manuscript.

Place	Date	Hour	Summary of Events and Information	Remarks and references to Appendices
LA BASTRE	2nd		54th Divisional Tactical Exercise No 2	
	3rd		176th Infantry Brigade Tactical Exercise No 2. 1 O.R. to Cooking Course	
	4th		Lt Newton from Leave. 1 O.R. to Rest Camp. 2 O.R. to Bombing Course.	
	6th		Divisional Field Day No 1.	
	11th		Divisional Tactical Exercise No 3	
	13th		Brigade Sports	
	16th		Coy Field firing Exercise	
	17th		Brigade Night Operations and dawn attack	
			2Lt BEATON & 4pl LEDDY reported from IX Corps Infantry School	
	22nd		Div'l Field Firing Exercise. 32 O.R. from 176 Inf Brigade attached to Coy.	
	23rd		Coy moved to BOUZINCOURT	
BOUZIN- COURT	24th		Major Burns from M.G. Course CAMIERS.	
	30th		Coy moved to WINNEZEELE.	
	31st		Strength 9 Coy. 188 (Officers 11 included), 32 O. attached	
			8 from 2/5 Lond Batty, 8 from 2/6 Lond Batty, 8 from 2/7 L 4 Staff, 8 from 2/8 L 4 Staff,	
			as Ammunition Carriers.	

Robt Burns
Capt
Comdg 9 C.L.R.

Army Form C. 2118.

WAR DIARY
or
INTELLIGENCE SUMMARY.

(Erase heading not required.)

Instructions regarding War Diaries and Intelligence Summaries are contained in F. S. Regs., Part II. and the Staff Manual respectively. Title pages will be prepared in manuscript.

Vol 8

Place	Date	Hour	Summary of Events and Information	Remarks and references to Appendices
			Original War Diary of 174th Machine Gun Company From:- Sept 1st 1917 To:- Sept 30th 1917	Confidential

WAR DIARY
or
INTELLIGENCE SUMMARY.

Army Form C. 2118.

Place	Date	Hour	Summary of Events and Information	Remarks and references to Appendices
WINNEZEELE	1/9/17		Gen. Remarks. 1 OR. to U.K. on leave.	
	2/9/17		Bde Church Parades. 2/Lt. DAY from leave to U.K.	
	3/9/17	7-7:30 9-12:30 2-3	Section Training. Barrage Drill, and Pack Saddle work. 1 OR. sick to Hospital.	
	4/9/17	9AM 1PM	Bde Tactical Scheme. 2 Sections working with Infantry — the attack. 2 " " " the Defence. 1 OR. sick evacuated to C.C.S	
	5/9/17	9-12:30 2-5PM	Sectn. Training. Scheme as above revised. Bde Tactical Scheme as above revised. 1 OR. to U.K. on leave, 1 OR. from "	
	6/9/17		Section Training. As above. 2/Lt. DODD and 1 OR. to course at 21st Squad. R.F.C. (3 days)	
	7/9/17	9AM to 2PM	Company Manl. Route, with Pack Transport, and Tactical Scheme, frarke in handling of M.G.s in Open Warfare in repel a cavalry tactics. 1 OR. to Div. Farrier's Course.	
	8/9/17		Section Training. 1 OR. Sick to Hosp. 1 OR. from "
	9/9/17		Bde Church Parade. 2/Lt. GILSHENAN to U.K. on leave (5 days) 4 ORs. to 21st Squad R.F.C. for course (5 days)	

Army Form C. 2118.

WAR DIARY
or
INTELLIGENCE SUMMARY.
(Erase heading not required.)

Instructions regarding War Diaries and Intelligence Summaries are contained in F. S. Regs., Part II and the Staff Manual respectively. Title pages will be prepared in manuscript.

Place	Date	Hour	Summary of Events and Information	Remarks and references to Appendices
WINNEZEELE	10/9/17	6 A.M. to 12 non-	Bde Route March – about 12 miles, without Transport. None fell out.	
	11/9/17		Sectn Shapeing Training. Lecture by 2/Lt DODD on "Moorlands" 1 O.R. sick to hospt 1 O.R. from Front.	
	12/9/17		Sectn Training. Barrage Work, & best Montage Drill. 1 O.R. to 2/Legion R.F.C. Gr. course.	
	13/9/17	10 A.M. to 2 P.M.	Company Tactical Scheme. Before D & S.O. to illustrate support to attack by the M.G. Barrage from 2 six gun Batteries and by consolidating guns (1 sectn) going forward for attack. (see attached "A") – Company captivated by D & S.O. Two an extraordinarily good show. Special good work of Signallers kept the scheme in running out lines rapidly to Batteries and to forward O.P. in the FRONT LINE. 1 O.R. on leave to U.K.	See Appendix A
	14/9/17	9.6. 12-30 2-3	Recoeve Practice on 30 yds Range. Sectn. Officers Class for NCOs 9 NCOs in Company work. LT NEWTON to Vet Corps course COLORS. 1 O.R. reported from Farmer's course.	

Army Form C. 2118.

WAR DIARY
or
INTELLIGENCE SUMMARY.
(Erase heading not required.)

Instructions regarding War Diaries and Intelligence Summaries are contained in F. S. Regs., Part II. and the Staff Manual respectively. Title pages will be prepared in manuscript.

Place	Date	Hour	Summary of Events and Information	Remarks and references to Appendices
WINNEZEELE	15/9/17.		Section Training	
	16/9/17.		MAJOR BEATTS to PARIS on 4 day leave.	
			Bde Church Parade.	
	17/9/17.		Bde Tactical Scheme. The Brigade, Infantry Battalion acting in attack and consolidation. M.G. Coy, T.M.B. the enemy. M.Gs well concealed and attacking tanks to observe their advance before consolidate positions approved.	
			2/Lt Brown leave to U.K.	
			1 OR to U.K. on leave.	
	18/9/17.		2 Gun Running Bathe.	
			Testing of all Box Respirators in the Gas Chamber.	
			2/LT K. BRECKENRIDGE to crash at 21st Sqnd. R.F.C. (3 days)	

Army Form C. 2118.

WAR DIARY
or
INTELLIGENCE SUMMARY.

(Erase heading not required.)

Place	Date	Hour	Summary of Events and Information	Remarks and references to Appendices
BRANDHOEK	19/9/17	11 A.M.	Company moved to BRANDHOEK. N°1 Bde to Lub. 1 O.R. (Sick) to Hospital.	
	20/9/17		Intra training.	
VLAMERTINGHE	21/9/17	9 P.M. 3 P.M.	Lt BURTON recc'naited night sector 55th Div. front. E of YPRES. Company moved to GOLDFISH CHATEAU, VLAMERTINGHE (S.I.11.a.5.2 – ref. sheet 28 BELGIUM 1/40,000) O.C. returned from leave to PARIS.	
	22/9/17	10 A.M. to 6 P.M.	O.C. 2/Lt DODD, 1 REDALE, CROCKER went out to recc'te line prepatory to relief of 164 & 165 M.G. Coys (55th Div) To Bde H.Q. WIELTJE (C.28.6.37) to arrange details of relief with these M.G. Coys. Sectors of the line. Bricks took Sector officers arrival. 176 Inf Bde relieved 164 & 165 Inf Bdes on the line. 2/Lt GILSHENAN returned from leave to U.K. Bde Hd. established at WIELTJE.	
	23/9/17	9 A.M. to 4 P.M.	D.M.S.O. MAJOR GRANT (O.C. 200 M.S.C) and self recc'naited the Div. front. Lt M.S. BUTLER travelled the barrage work to support our and to support attack. Recc'te was made by the DIXSEN attacking on a two Brigade front. 178 Inf Bde on the right, 176 Inf Bde on left "Sectn". 177 Inf Bde in support. Two Guns (1 sectn) from each attacking Bde M.G. Coy be attached respectively to the company and 200 S.G. for Barrage work. Two Guns of 20 Guns each thus formed in each attacking Brigade area. MAJOR BENNS appointed O.C. L Group. MAJOR GRANT O.C. R Group.	

Army Form C. 2118.

WAR DIARY
or
INTELLIGENCE SUMMARY.
(Erase heading not required.)

Instructions regarding War Diaries and Intelligence Summaries are contained in F. S. Regs., Part II. and the Staff Manual respectively. Title pages will be prepared in manuscript.

Place	Date	Hour	Summary of Events and Information	Remarks and references to Appendices
E YPRES	23/24 9/17		Relief of 164 & 165 M.G. Companies in the front line 55th Div. front. No 2 and No 4 Sectns in right Sectn, with Sectn HQ at POMMERN CASTLE (D.19.a.47.4) No 1 and No 3 Sectns in left Sectn, with Sectn HQ at SOMME dug-out (D.13.d.1.6) and SCHULER GALLERIES (D.13.a.6.5) respectively. For disposition of guns of the Company see Appendix "B" map. — Company HQ at Pill Box KIELTJE (D.13.a.6.5)	See Appendix "B"
GRAVENSTAFEL and FREZENBURG Sheet 1:10,000	24/9/17	7 P.M.	Relief complete 7 PM.	
		10 A.M.	Reconnaissance by Battery Junrs of 1st Group made by MAJOR BEARS and Battery Commanders. 2/Lt DODD & No 1 Sectn wiped at SOMME. 2/Lt W.J. BEATON wiped and killed by gun shot wound. Arth (R) Battery parties show as follows:—	2. O.R.s to Hospital
			D Battery C.13.c.15.65. E " C.13.a.30.50. F " C.18.6.98.50.	
		12 noon	Casualties Keeled Killed 2/Lt W.J. BEATON. Transport moved up to BRICKFIELDS VLAMERTINGHE.	
			Wounded. 1 OR. 4 ORs. 2 ORs from Div. Reinforcements Bn.	
	24/25		176 Inf Bde relieved by 178 Inf Bde in left Sectn and "77 Inf Bde in right Sub-Sectn, Preparatory to attack on the 26th inst. 176 Inf Bde to Support, one R. Kent in Support of each Bde in reserve at GOLD FISH CHATEAU V.	

Army Form C. 2118.

WAR DIARY
or
INTELLIGENCE SUMMARY.
(Erase heading not required.)

Instructions regarding War Diaries and Intelligence Summaries are contained in F.S. Regs., Part II. and the Staff Manual respectively. Title pages will be prepared in manuscript.

Place	Date	Hour	Summary of Events and Information	Remarks and references to Appendices
	25/9/17	9 P.M.	Company relieved by 175 M.S. Co. in Left Sector, and by 177 M.S. Co. in Right Sector. - On relief Sections proceeded to POND SAUER 155 (N3 8 b 6.) and SPREE FARM Hutches (C.18.d.2.2.4.). N.1. Section 175 M.S. Co. under 2/Lt. J.H. HOBSON attached to Coy. Barrage, reported and accommodated at SPREE FARM. Relief Complete.	
		12 Mdnt	During night of 24/25. N.1. Section 175 M.S. Co. (F Battery) dug gun pits at Battery Position and placed in Cupola. Section Sgt 14 M.S. Co. on reky. carried guns ammn. etc to above relative Battery Position on Mule R.T. no difficulty experienced. Detailed orders for attack received and N.S. Barrage Programme. See Appendix C. GRAVENSTAFEL MAP showing our own front line and 1st - 2nd Objectives, Divisional Boundaries, Zones of Batteries of Lt. Group and Targets. See also Appendix "D". The Barrage Tables (worked out by Battery Commander at Coy. H.Q. SIETZTJE in afternoon and checked by Group Command and D.M.S.O.	See Appendix "C" Appendix "D"
		9 P.M.	Batteries began taking up positions, completed by 2 A.M. GROUP H.Q. established at POND SPLUEGES (C.18.c.8.12.) in Liason with 178 Inf. Bde H.Q. at CAPRICORN KEEP (C.18.a.5.6.) Rt. GROUP H.Q. at POTTSERN REDOUBT in Liason with 177 Inf Bde H.Q. at BANK FARM (C.24.V.3.5.)	

A7092 Wt. W128 9/M1293 750,000. 1/17. D. D. & L., Ltd. Forms/C2118/14.

WAR DIARY or INTELLIGENCE SUMMARY

Army Form C. 2118.

Place	Date	Hour	Summary of Events and Information	Remarks and references to Appendices
	25/9/16		Work of troops up S.A.A. to Battery positions and dumps of SROUP DUMP at SPREE FARM under C.S.M. "A" M.S.G.	
	26/9/17	2AM	Work completed by 2AM and telephone communication established with Batteries	1 Lt NEWTON from Neg. (once CALAIS), etc. to U.K. on leave.
		4AM	Tanks - their Crews up to trenches to attack.	
		5.50AM	ZERO HOUR.	
			Whole Artillery Barrage inc. From ZERO - 2 hrs. At ZERO, including 38 Heavy and Siege Batteries. The Army Batteries fired a Divisional & Corps Artillery	See Appendix "E"
			14 TANKS got up during the night and commenced gas "+ shelter at ZERO. For detailed report on the attack see Appendix "E". This deals with the attack from the M.S.G. point of view.	
	27/9/17	8AM	Order received from D.M.S.O. to withdraw GROUP to CORP RESERVE TRENCH. Carried into effect. Gp HQ. Established at C.23.c.5.6 (C.23.c.)	
			2/Lts IREDALE & CROCKER sent back to TRANSPORT LINE	
		4PM	Messages received from D.M.S.O. to select position for, and place - also by 8TH, & 9TH Battery to cover with S.O.S. Range assigned 58 Zie Co. on left Bank to the lake, we by 59" Division that night.	
			Be at (1st DAY positions at, reported party to Battery at FORT HILL C.18.C.23.46) Covering the our front between - WINZIG to D.8.d.6.0.	

Army Form C. 2118.

WAR DIARY
or
INTELLIGENCE SUMMARY.
(Erase heading not required.)

Instructions regarding War Diaries and Intelligence Summaries are contained in F. S. Regs., Part II. and the Staff Manual respectively. Title pages will be prepared in manuscript.

Place	Date	Hour	Summary of Events and Information	Remarks and references to Appendices
	27/9/17	10 P.M.	2/Lt. DAY, NEWTON and 8 Gun Battery on Battery and on S.O.S. lines at FORT HILL.	
			Heavy bombardment around Battery position at dusk and dawn 28/9/17. Casualties killed 1 O.R. wounded 3 O.Rs.	
	28/9/17	10 P.M. to 3 A.M.	M.G. Corps in Action. (175 & 177 M.S. Coys) assisted by D.H.S.O. and O.C.C5. No shortage of Barrage fire being required. Battery relieved & position as usual.	
		3 P.M.	S.O.S. Barrage of FORT HILL Battery narrowed to 200 yds either side of road running E from costal ship on C5. 5"(Dn) M.S. Coy to arrange for relief on night of 30th in Sheu Battery positions.	
		6 P.M.	BOETLEER (D.8 cen.kat) and 30Y in front Bon Bernthe.	
	29/9/17	10 A.M.	2/Lt. A.N. DODD from C5 H.Q. relieved 2/Lt P.H. NEWTON with Battery. Battery proceed relieved by front men from CORPS RESERVE TRENCH. 2 N.C.O.s & M.S. Corps carriers 2/Lt NEWTON to Transport lines.	
		12 noon		
		4 P.M.	Remainder of company and H.Q. Staff 175 M.S. Coy proceeded with Kit to Transport lines.	
		6 P.M.	2 officers & 8 ORs 5"(Dn) No. 2 M.S. Coy arrived for alternate Battery relief and a schedule.	
	30/9/17	10 A.M.	1 Officer & 4 ORs to FORT HILL to take ob. and see LT GROUP area. Remainder shown R.T. GROUP area by 2/LT ZILSHENNAN and an officer of the R.T. BARRAGE GROUP.	

WAR DIARY
or
INTELLIGENCE SUMMARY

Army Form C. 2118.

Place	Date	Hour	Summary of Events and Information	Remarks and references to Appendices
	30/9/17	8 P.M. to 10 P.M.	Relief of Company by 5th (Div.) N.Z. M.S. Company complete 10 P.M. On relief Company proceeded to Transport lines. Relief of 5/9th Division by 1st New-Zealand Division complete. Strength of Company: Officers 9, Other Ranks 152. Total Casualties: Killed 2/Lt W.T. BEATON, 7 other ranks. Wounded 2/Lt W. BRECKENRIDGE, 19 other ranks. Missing believed Killed 2 other ranks.	

J. McField
30.9.17

R. Benny Capt
Cmdg 174th Machine Gun Coy

Secret.
ref.Sht 27
1/40000

Appendix
174 Machine Gun Company

[Stamp: ORDERLY ROOM / Date / No. recd 15/9/17 / 174 M.G. COMPANY]

O. O. No 2.

Action of our own Troops

1. Two small States EASTLAND & WESTLAND have declared War. The Frontier is the Stream RAU D'HERZEELE flowing through D.28.d.23.d.17 to the North in which EASTLAND has taken up defensive positions.

On the 12/9/17 Westland attacked Eastland on their left a Southern flank and established a line about 200 yards East of the road running through D.29.d.

176th Inf Bde are disposed at dawn on the 13/9/17 as follows:-

2/5th South Staff on a frontage of 300 yards dug in from approximately D.29.d.2.8½ to D.29.d.7.2.
Two Companies in Front Line. Two Companies in Support.
The 2/6th Staff (South) in Support disposed in Artillery formation Shell holes about D.29.d.0.8.

One Section 174 M.G. Coy is in position in our front System to support these 2 Btn.

Touch has been established with the 177th Bde on our left and 178th Bde on our right.

Information has been received that the enemy are holding strong points at about D.30.c.0.8. and D.30.a.0.1. Strength about one Company, strong points on road about D.30.a.5.0. and D.30.a.3.5.

Strength about one Company. It has been decided that the Bde shall attack at 10.15 am. 2/5th South Staff Regt will capture and consolidate strong point D.30.c.0.8. and D.30.a.0.1. as 1st objective and strong point D.30.a.5.0. and D.30.a.3.5. on road as 2nd objective, moving behind Artillery Barrage (See appendix A.)

Battle Outposts will be pushed forward to BOIS ST ACAIRE, to ascertain if enemy has evacuated when Artillery Barrage ceases at 11.30 am.

2/6th South Staff Regt will remain about D.29.d.0.8 and will be prepared to support the 2/5th South Staff in their advance and to Counter Attack immediately should the enemy succeed in re-capturing any portion of the captured positions.

Sheet 2.

2. **Action of Machine Gun Company**

The 174th M.G. Coy will support the attack as follows:-

(A) No 1 Section will go forward with the 2/5th South Staff and assist in the consolidation, disposing guns so as to bring crossfire to flank each strong point captured (See appendix B)

(B) Remainder of the Guns of the Company will be formed into 2 Batteries each of 6 Guns as follows:-

A. Battery No. 2 Section 2 Guns No 4.
at about J.4.d.1.4. Sector Battery Commander
2/Lt H.M. DAY

B. Battery No 3 Section 2 Guns No 4.
at about J.4.a.7.5. Sector. Battery Commander.
2/Lt W.H. IREDALE

These Batteries will assist the Infantry during the advance by a creeping frontal Barrage and will be prepared to protect them during and after consolidation by putting down a protective S.O.S. Barrage, 200 yards in front of the final objective (see appendix C) Fire Organization Table for these Batteries).

The Div M.G. Coy are arranging for Standing Barrages to be placed at the Strong Points.

3. Communications will be by telephone and runners, those going forward will send back messages to Advanced Company Report Centre at D.29.d.4.3. to which place also Visual Signalling will be established.

Telephone messages can be sent from Bde Battle H.Q. via Btn H.Q. on the line and these will be transmitted to Coy H.Q.

A & B Batteries will be in telephone communication with Company H.Q. under arrangements to be made by this Office

4. Coy H.Q will be at J.4.c.1.2. Advanced Report Centre at D.29.d.4.3. Bde H.Q. will be at J.4.c.1.4.

5. Dumps there will be an Advanced Dump for Gun going forward at D.29.c.9.7 to include 20,000 rounds S.A.A. Water. Spare parts, tools and sand bags

Main Dump and for Batteries at J.4.c.1.3 to include 70,000 rounds S.A.A. 24 gallons Water & Spareparts.

Indents on Main dump from N.C.O i/c Advanced Dump will be dealt with by Pack Transport.

Sheet 3.

cont⁰

5. 8 Yukon Packs will be dumped at the Advanced Dump and will be used by Section Carriers up to the forward Guns. Officer Commanding No 1 Section will detail N.C.O i/c of the forward Dump.
Cyclist Communication between Main and Forward Dump will be arranged by this Office.

6. Watches will be synchronised at 8. A.m. by Officers at Coy H Q.

7. Transport arrangements. T.O. will detail 8 pack mules to convey Guns of N⁰ 1 Section into assembly positions. They will then return to Main Dump to await orders.
8 additional mules will be left ready to move off at a moment's notice at J. 11. d. 7 9.
T.O will arrange for Dump to be kept supplied as required by Coy H.Q.

Appendix B

Guns going forward.
(1) Guns will form up on our Front Line prior to going over.
(2) And will be in position by Zero - 30 minutes
(3) Ready to kick off at Zero + 30 minutes.
(4) Route to follow will be E of Wood thro' D. 29. c. d. and to 200. Yards W. of Stream when they will follow the course S.E. From this dead ground the exact positions to be taken up can be reconnoitred and guns guided direct into positions.
(5) 2 Guns under 2/Lt A. N. DODD will arrange to flank the posts at D. 30. C. 0. 8. and D 30. a. 0. 1. from positions at about D. 29 b 3. 2 and D. 30 C 0. 6. and 2 Guns under 2/Lt. BEATON. W. J. Lt flank Posts at D 30. a. 5. 0. D 30. 2. 3. 5. for positions about D 30. 8. 2. 3 and D 30. C. 4. 8.

Appendix A

Artillery lifts 100 yards at a time as follows:-

    Commences on stream   10.15 am
    First lift   10.18 am
    Second lift   10.22 am
    Third lift, on to road   10.30 am
    Fourth lift, off road   11.0 am

Forms a Protective Barrage on West edge of BOIS ST ACAIRE till 11.30 am.
It will then cease unless S.O.S. is required.

Appendix "B"

    The Organisation Orders for Batteries.

                                               [signature]
                                               Capt.
                                    Comdg 174th Machine Gun Co.

Appendix B

1:10 000   K.3.   EDITION I.   Parts of 28 N.E. / 28 N.W.

55 Div Boundaries, taken ove by 59 Div 22/23.8.17
—— Bde Boundary
= M.G. positions taken ove by 174 M.G.Cy from 164 & 165 M.G. Cys 23/24
= Sector H.Q.

Message Form.

..................Division.

Map reference or mark own position on Map at back.

1. I am at..

2. I am at..and am consolidating.

3. I am at..and have consolidated.

4. I need :—Ammunition.
    Bombs.
    Rifle Grenades.
    Water.
    Very lights.
    Stokes shells.

5. Enemy forming up for counter-attack at..

6. I am in touch with........................on Right / Left at........................

7. I am not in touch on Right / Left

8. Am being shelled from..

9. I estimate my present strength at..rifles.

10. Hostile { Battery / Machine Gun / Trench Mortar } active at........................

Time........................a.m. (p.m.)   Name........................

Date........................   Platoon................ Company............

Place........................   Battalion........................

Appendix "D"

Ref. S.37
GCEWENSTAFEL Sheet
1:10,000

FIRE ORGANISATION ORDERS.

Battery. D **Place.** ___ **Date.** 26.9.17.

Composition. No.[?] 24th [?] 174 M.G. Co. **Frontage of Battery.** 70' **Tasks.** A_1 = D.8.a.2; A_2 = OTTO FARM
Commanded by 2/Lt. T.S. SILSHENAN. **Grid Bearing to R.O.** ___ B = D.15.b.w.
Location of Directing Gun. D.13.c.15.65 **Zero Line from D.13.c.15.65 through D.8.a.55** C = S.O.S.
No. of Directing Gun. 8 **Grid Bearing of Zero Line.** 61°

Barrage.	No. of guns.	Targets.	Clock time.	Zero time.	Deviation from Zero Line.	Distri-bution Angle.	Range.	V.I. by metres	Q.E.	Range to F.T. when Barrage lifts	Clearance when Bar-rage lifts	Rate of Fire.
A_1	4	D.8.D.2	0'6"+ 1h.40m.		0°	3°10'	1900	+6	4°			180 /Gn [?]
B.	8	D.15.b.w.	+2 hrs to +4 hrs		13°R	40'	2500	+13	7°45'			50 "
C.(S.O.S)	8	D.15.a.17.47 D.15.a.66.80	+4 hrs minutes		17°30'R	10'	see "Remarks"					
		In A_2 Task No 9 Directing Gun is Nu.4										
A_2	4	OTTO FARM	0'6"+ 1h.40m.		21°R	30'	2000	+2	4°20'			75 /Gn [?]

	8	7	6	5	4	3	2	1		Remarks.
A_1	0°	3°10'	6°20'	9°30'						This shews angle from Zero line for each gun. From this line barrage chart for each gun is compiled and issued to Gun Commanders.
B.	13°R	13°40'	14°20'	15°	15°40'	16°20'	17°	17°40'		
C.	17°30'R	17°40'	17°50'	18°	18°10'	18°20'	18°30'	18°40'		
A_2					21°R	21°30'	22°	22°30'		

C (S.O.S)   Q.Es.

R	7	6	5	4	3	2	1
4°39'	4°51'	5°3'	5°13'	5°27'	5°39'	5°51'	6°5'

Ref. GRAVENSTAFEL Sheet
1:10,000

FIRE ORGANISATION ORDERS.

Battery. **E** Place.
Date. 26.9.17.

Composition. N.3 Section Subsection N.2 Sect. 174 H.B.y Frontage of Battery. 50y Tasks. A = D.15.c.20.15
Commanded by 2/Lt K.H. IREDALE Grid Bearing to R.O.   B = D.15.a.x
Location of Directing Gun. C.13.a.30.60. Zero Line from C.13.a.30.00 through D.15.c.00.40] C = S.O.S.
No. of Directing Gun. 6. Grid Bearing of Zero Line. 107°

Barrage.	No. of guns.	Targets.	Clock time.	Zero time.	Deviation from Zero Line.	Distribution Angle.	Range.	V.I.	Q.E.	Range to F.T. when Barrage lifts	Clearance when Barrage lifts	Rate of Fire.
A.	6	D.15.c.20.15		0%+47 mins	0°	50'	2050	nil	4°50'			60 rpm
B.	6	D.15.a.x		0%+52 mins to 0%+55	24'L	1°	2250	+10	5°5'			50 "
C. (S.O.S)	6	D.14.b.85.75 to D.15.a.20.50		+4 hrs onwards	23'L	1°	See Remarks					

Remarks.

C (S.O.S)   Q.Es.

This shows angle from Zero line for each gun. From this line barrage chart for each gun is compiled and issued to Gun Commanders.

	8	7	6	5	4	3	2	1
A.		—	0°	50'R	1°40'	2°30'	3°20'	4°10'
B.		—	24'L	23°	22°	21°	20°	19°
C.(S.O.S)		—	23'L	22°	21°	20°	19°	18°
			3°38'	3°46	3°52	3°52'	4°2'	4°10'	4°20

S.37

Ref. S.37

FIRE ORGANISATION ORDERS.

Map. GRAVENSTAFEL Sheet 1/10,000. Battery. F   Place.   Date. 26.9.17.

Composition. N¹ Sub¹ 175 M.G. ¹st Sub¹ 174 M.G. Frontage of Battery. 50ʸ Tasks. A = VAN ISACKERS FARM
Commanded by 2Lt W.H. Hobson. Grid Bearing to R.O.   B = D.9.c.Y.
Location of Directing Gun. E.18.t.48.50. Zero line from E.18.t.4650 through D.19.25.75 C = S.O.S.
N². of Directing gun. 6   Grid Bearing of Zero Line. 114°

Barrage.	No. of guns.	Targets.	Clock time.	Zero time.	Deviation from Zero line.	Distribution Angle.	Range.	V.I.	Q.E.	Range to F.T. when Barrage lifts	Clearance when Barrage lifts range	Rate of fire.
A.	6	VAN ISACKERS FARM	0/6 +8mins		0°	10'	2350	+10	6°36'			80 P.h.
B.	6	D.9.c.Y.	+10m¹ +4hrs		38°L	1°10'	2100	+12	5°8'			50 ,,
C (SOS)	6	D.8.d.65.00 to D.14.t.85.75	+4hr. onwds		32°L	50'	1900	+5	3°58'			

	8	7	6	5	4	3	2	1
A.			0°	0° 10'R	20'	30'	40'	50'
B.			38°L	36°50	35°40	34°30	33°20	32°10
C.			32°L	31°10	30°20	29°30	28°40	27°50

Remarks.
This shews angle from Zero line for each gun. From this line barrage chart for each gun is compiled and issued to Gun Commanders.

174 Machine Gun Company   Appendix C

Report on Recent Operations E. of YPRES
26-27 September 1917

Ref. GRAVENSTAFEL } Sheets 1:10,000
    FREZENBURG

Reconnaissance was necessarily slight and hurried.
The Company relieved 164 & 165 M.G. Coy in front line positions on night of 23/24 Sept. Relief complete at 7.5 AM
On the morning of 23rd a reconnaissance of the line was made by D.M.G.O. Major Grant (OC R. BARRAGE GROUP) and self. This was practically confined to right subsection. Localities for positions of Batteries of Lt Group were marked on the map by D.M.G.O.
During morning of 24th O.C. Coy and Battery Commanders reconnoitred the Lt Sub Sector through glasses from POND GALLERIES and positions for Batteries were chosen as follows:—

D Battery   C.13.C.15.65.
   Consisting of No 1 & 4 Sections 174 M.G. Coy.
   Commanded by 2/LT T.S. GILSHENAN.

E Battery   C.13.a 30.00.
   Consisting of No 3 Section & one subsection
   No 2 Section 174 M.G. Coy
   Commanded by 2/LT W.H. IREDALE

F Battery   C.18.b 98.50
   Consisting of No 1 Section 175 M.G. Coy
   & one Subsection of No 2 Section 174 M.G. Coy
   Commanded by 2/LT J H HOBSON

All these Battery positions being 400-500 yds from the front line and in full view of the enemy it was impossible to dig in or allow any movement by day near the positions. Also the Company was not relieved in the line until the night of 24/25th.   Company relieved by
   175 M.G. Coy in left Sub Sector
   177 M.G. Coy in right sub sector.
Relief not complete till 8 A.M. 25th
Owing to malmanagements in relief and difficulties arising, no work could be done on Battery positions during night of 24/25 except in the case of F Battery, (1 Section 175 M.G. Coy) who were fresh troops coming straight in. They dug their guns in, put tripods

in position. On relief, Sections proceeded to SPREE FARM and POND GALLERIES. During 25th work of preparation was continued. Ammunition, spare parts, & water etc were carried up as near to Battery positions as was compatible with a degree of safety.

At noon, programme for M.G Barrages was received and Fire Organisation Table, Barrage Charts, and Fighting maps were drawn up by Battery Commanders at Company H.Q WIELTJE (Bde H.Q dug out) and checked by GROUP Commander.

Supply of S.A.A On nights of 24/25 & 25/26 100,000 S.A.A were brought up under Company arrangements and dumped at SPREE FARM which was made the Main Group dump under C.S.M 174 M.G. Coy. 300,000 S.A.A for M.G's of the Group was also brought up and dumped in the same locality by arrangements made with 176 Inf Bde carrying party.

Company HQrs and Communications Coy H.Q was established at 8.PM 25th at POND GALLERIES. C.18.6.8.1½ from which E & F Batteries (only 200 - 300 yds to the left & right front), could be observed. Telephonic Communication was opened with all 3 Batteries. Also to 178 Inf Bde at CAPRICORN KEEP through whom it was possible to get on to D.M.G.O at advanced Div H.Q. WIELTJE dug out.

All Batteries were dug in, and deep slits provided for teams by 2 AM. The following S.A.A was up with the Batteries:—

      D Battery   60,000 rounds & 20 belt boxes per gun.

      E Battery   42,000 rounds & 16 belt boxes per gun

      F Battery   35,000 rounds & 14 belt boxes per gun

Belt filling arrangements by hand up in shell holes with the Battery and by Machine in POND GALLERIES (for E & F Batteries) and in pill box at C.18.d.8.5½ for D Battery.

ZERO DAY
MORNING

Hostile bombardment   From 3.15 AM to 5.45 AM the enemy barraged alight over the Area occupied by the Batteries. But in spite of this at Zero there were no casualties this good result was due entirely to the excellent digging in of all Batteries. The men lay at the bottom of their slits and direct hits on Gun positions only resulted in the burying of the teams.

Zero Hour   5.30 AM. The M.G programme was opened and carried through without a hitch. The Guns fired wonderfully and the men were in excellent spirits.   7.48 AM detailed report made to D.M.G.O by runner.   At 9.40 AM report made to 178 Bde HQ to this effect.

After 9 AM enemy's barrage which had shortened. Lengthened again on to old barrage lines across our Batteries. Three guns were knocked out and teams buried but casualties were slight before Noon.

At 12 Noon Message received from D.M.G.O. suspected enemy Counter attack on 58th Div front on our left. Order to barrage D.8.a.3. Central in a line with word GRAVENSTAFEL passed to Batteries over phone to E and F Batteries and by Orderly to D Battery.

Fire opened at 12.5 PM on new target and maintained for half an hour after which guns laid on SOS lines again.

AFTERNOON   Heavy bombardment of Battery positions during the afternoon.   E & F Batteries suffering most heavily. Guns and teams several times buried and casualties inflicted, but all ranks stuck to their guns splendidly.

At 4.40 PM message received from D.M.G.O to maintain fire on D.9.C.t.5. (GRAVENSTAFEL CROSS ROADS) communicated to Batteries and rate of fire a belt per gun per hour ordered.

5.35 PM   estimated Casualties
<u>Killed 4 OR's</u>
Wounded 20 OR's

5.45 PM Bad times for E & F Batteries who had only 4 Guns left in working order. Impossible to mount guns of F Battery because of annihilating bombardment, guns therefore placed at the bottom of the slits and teams of F Battery withdrawn to shelter behind POND GALLERIES for a breather. D & E Batteries still in action and firing on D.9.C.Y

ENEMY COUNTER ATTACK

Enemy counter Attack

At 6.30 PM enemy counter attacked in mass and the S O S went up. Fire at once opened by E & D Batteries on their S.O.S lines; reports of Infantry in our front line state, this fire was down before the Artillery, and was successful in breaking up the Boch formation. Almost immediately supports seemed to be retiring from the direction of SCHULER GALLERIES between which and front line the enemy's Barrage was very heavy. By this time E & F Batteries were practically blown up. As the situation was not clear I decided to rally on the line POND GALLERIES and organised it as a defence line. Four guns were salved from the blown up Batteries and got into position along POND GALLERIES. With conspicuous gallantry 2nd Lts HOBSON and BRACKENRIDGE volunteered to go out to F Battery to salve the first gun. BRACKENRIDGE was hit but HOBSON went right through the Barrage for 200 yds with Sigt SALMON and brought in a gun and tripod. The remaining 3 guns were brought in when the Barrage lifted back.

MAJOR PRATT and 2 Companies of the 2/8" N.D's then came up and reinforced this line. I arranged with him to send forward 2 M.G.s under 2/LT J.T CROCKER with these Companies. At 7.30 I received a message from MAJOR PRATT stating that the 2/7" N.D's were in front of him still holding the 2nd Objective TORONTO LINE. Two more guns dug out from E Battery position to go forward to SCHULER GALLERIES.

Message received from D.M.G.O at 8.30 P.M. that infantry were retiring in our centre at about HILL 35. Order to dismount all barrage guns and mount for direct fire on best line across Div front. Suggested line HINDU COTT — AISNE FARM — SOMME — POMMERN CASTLE.

But by this time the situation was clear.

2/LT P.H. NEWTON from D Battery arrived with MAJOR PRATT's party in Command of a company of these stragglers and went across to D Battery for 2nd LT T.S. GILSHENAN. who handed over there to 2nd LT A.N. DODD

GILSHENAN then reported that infantry supports did also retire on his Battery and on C Battery Rt Group on his right but he forced them to rally on the line of his Battery threatening to turn his guns on them if they did not comply. He then organised the stragglers into Sections under what N.C.O's that remained put likely looking privates in charge too. Thus reorganised and brought up against the Batteries the wavering troops went up again, to their old positions but recently vacated. Reinforcements similarly passed through this Battery and the situation thus righted itself. This did not necessitate a readjustment of guns in depth as ordered by D.M.G.O and my action was approved by him. Steady fire was meanwhile maintained by D Battery.

Things quietened down considerably by 9.30 P.M and the night was very quiet.

This was particularly fortunate as the men were by this time very shaken and exhausted by the strain of sticking to the guns. And every effort was made to rest the teams during the night leaving only one man per gun on duty as sentry.

At 3 A.M. 27th message was received from D.M.G.O to withdraw the Group to Corps Reserve Trench (C.23.a) for reorganisation and rest.

This was done at 8 A.M.

<u>Total Casualties</u> Killed 5 ORs
Wounded 2LT W. BRACKENRIDGE
" 20 ORs
Missing 2 ORs
believed killed
Total 1 and 27

Number of Rounds fired 230,000

Before leaving the Battery areas and **SCHULER GALLERIES** careful search was made to salve all guns, tripods and kit, these were taken back to Corps Reserve Trench during the morning, also knocked out guns.

Total Guns knocked out 4
" Tripods " " 4

Number Guns brought out of the line 20
" Tripods " " " " 19

These additional guns were salved from the battlefield also several belt boxes found lying about.

<u>Esprit de Corps</u>. Throughout the whole attack the spirit of the men was excellent. They stuck to their guns as a matter of course, and though wounded had in several instances to be definitely ordered by an Officer to go down. The supply of ammunition and filled belt boxes never ran short and the carriers kept up a constant supply though it meant them going through a heavy barrage to the guns.

The men were confident of success and trusted their guns implicitly. They dug in splendidly on Y night well knowing that in that lay their safety and they were right.

The reported good results of the barrage fire have bucked the gunners up no end, and there is no doubt that if proper precautions are taken in concealment and cover M.G. Batteries can remain in position during annihilating bombardment and come into action at the desired moment with momentous effect.

Leslie P Berry
Capt
174 K.S.Co.
Cmdg L.T Barrage Group

Army Form C. 2118.

WAR DIARY
or
INTELLIGENCE SUMMARY
(Erase heading not required.)

Vol 9

Confidential

Original War Diary
of
114th Machine Gun Company

From 2nd Oct 1917
To 31st Oct 1917.

Army Form C. 2118.

WAR DIARY
or
INTELLIGENCE SUMMARY.

(Erase heading not required.)

Instructions regarding War Diaries and Intelligence
Summaries are contained in F. S. Regs., Part II.
and the Staff Manual respectively. Title pages
will be prepared in manuscript.

Place	Date	Hour	Summary of Events and Information	Remarks and references to Appendices
	2/10/17		Company entrained for TREZENNES. 2 O.R. to Hospital	
	3	7.30 a.m.	arrived at TREZENNES 2 O.R. to C.C.S.	
	4		Major BENNS to U.K. for duty in AMERICA.	
	5		2/Lt HARDY. S. joined Company from Base	
	6		33 O.R.	
	7		Company entrained for VERCHIN	
	8		Lt STEWART A.J. from 232 M.G Coy joined Company as O.C.	
	9		1 O.R. joined Company from Base 1 O.R. from 46 S STAFFS attached as Cinner	
	10		Company embussed for FOSSE 10. PT SAINS	
			2/Lt DAY + 2/Lt IREDALE reconnoitred line. LENS sector	
	11		Capt STEWART " " " " "	
	12		Company relieved 2nd CANADIAN M.G Coy in LENS sector	
			Lt BURTON to U.K. for 6 months duty in ENGLAND	
	13		night of 12/13 1500 rounds fired on Enemys communications in + around LENS	
			13/14 16,480	
	14		2/Lt BRACKENRIDGE rejoined Company from Base	

WAR DIARY or INTELLIGENCE SUMMARY

Army Form C. 2118.

Place	Date	Hour	Summary of Events and Information	Remarks and references to Appendices
LENS Sector	15.10.17		Night of 14/15. 12,380 rounds fired on Enemy communications in & around LENS. H.A. guns fired 1000 rounds on E.A.	
	16		Night of 15/16 14,600 rounds on normal night targets. 750 rounds on E.A.	
	17		16/17 12,070 "	
	18		17/18 14,170 " 500 rounds on E.A.	
	19		18/19 13,500 "	
			Two new guns put in position for defence of Red line.	
		5.15 p.m.	S.O.S. sent up. Guns fired 6,500	
	20		Night of 19/20 11,500 rounds fired on normal night targets	
			Strength increase week ending 20.10.17. 19 O.R. 2 O.R. attached	
			Strength decrease week ending 20.10.17. 3 O.R. 1 O.R. attached	
		11.1 p.m.	15,250 rounds fired on special target N.20.d.92 LENS 36.5 S.W.1	
	21		Night of 20/21 6000 rounds on normal night targets	
			200 M.G. Coy relieved 174 M.G. Coy in the line. Company on relief proceeded to CARENCY	Sheet 36 & 36a70
CARENCY	23		2/Lt CROCKER & 56 OR to MARQUEFFLES FARM to work on field firing range R26.L.	"
			2/Lt DODD to UK on leave	
	24–27		Improvement of Camp. Sectional training.	

WAR DIARY
or
INTELLIGENCE SUMMARY.

(Erase heading not required.)

Army Form C. 2118.

Place	Date	Hour	Summary of Events and Information	Remarks and references to Appendices
CARENCY	27.10.17		Strength increase during week ending 27.10.17 2. OR. 1 OR attached	
			Strength decrease during week ending 27.10.17 1. OR	
	29.30		Sectional training	
	31		Company route march.	
			Strength of Company	
			Officers OR	
			10 198	
			31 attached	
			229	

In the field. 31.10.17

TS Pritchard 2/Lt.
a/adj 174 M.G.Coy

Army Form C. 2118.

Vol 10

Confidential

WAR DIARY
or
INTELLIGENCE SUMMARY.
(Erase heading not required.)

War Diary
of
171st Machine Gun Company
1st to 30th Nov 1917

Place	Date	Hour	Summary of Events and Information	Remarks and references to Appendices

Original

Army Form C. 2118.

WAR DIARY
or
INTELLIGENCE SUMMARY.
(Erase heading not required.)

Instructions regarding War Diaries and Intelligence Summaries are contained in F.S. Regs., Part II. and the Staff Manual respectively. Title pages will be prepared in manuscript.

174 Machine Gun Company
Month of November 1917

Place	Date	Hour	Summary of Events and Information	Remarks and references to Appendices
CARENCY	1/11/17 to 2		Sectional training {Strength increase week ending 3/11/17	
	3/11/17		{Strength decrease week ending 3/11/17	
	4/11/17		Captain A.J. STEWART requisitioned large AVION sector with reference relief 7/8/11/17. 2ND LT A.N. DODD returned from leave to U.K.	
	5/11/17		All sector officers reconnoitred line	
	6/11/17		2ND LT P.H. NEWTON proceeded on Artillery course	
			Preparations for relief	
			2ND LT J.T. CROCKER and 56 O.R. returned from keeping long machine gun range at MARQUEFFLES FARM	
AVION	7/11/17	8 p.m.	Relieved 175 Machine Gun Company in AVION sector	
	8/11/17		1,600 rounds fired on enemy aircraft	
	9/11/17		12,875 rounds expended harassing fire on enemy's communications during night of 8/9th	
	10/11/17	2 a.m.	15,875 rounds fired on special targets for a raid that was to have taken place - raid cancelled owing to non-appearance of Brigade torpedo during night of 9/10th harassing fire - 13,375 rounds expended - on report of enemy massing for attack at gun's laid @ SOS lines - 5,500 rounds fired at above rate {Strength decrease week ending 10/11/17 = 2 in reserve { " increase " " 10/11/17 = 4	
	11/11/17		2,350 rounds fired on enemy aircraft during night of 11/12th 9,500 rounds expended harassing fire on enemy's communications	
	12/11/17		during night of 11/12th 12,550 rounds expended in harassing fire	

WAR DIARY
or
INTELLIGENCE SUMMARY.

(Erase heading not required.)

Army Form C. 2118.

Instructions regarding War Diaries and Intelligence Summaries are contained in F. S. Regs., Part II. and the Staff Manual respectively. Title pages will be prepared in manuscript.

Place	Date	Hour	Summary of Events and Information	Remarks and references to Appendices
AVION SECTOR	13/11/17		During night of 12/13th 12,500 rounds fired on enemy's communications	
	14/11/17		During night of 13/14th 16,500 rounds fired on enemy's communications	
	15/11/17		" " 14/15th 14,500 " " "	
	16/11/17		100 rounds fired on enemy aircraft. During night of 15/16th 8,000 rounds fired on enemy's communications. 250 rounds fired on enemy aircraft	
	17/11/17		During night 16/17th 9,750 rounds fired on enemy's communications. Strength decrease during week ending 17/11/17 8 increase " " " " 17/11/17 1 Casualties 2 O.R. wounded. During night 17/18th company relieved in AVION SECTOR by 3rd Canadian M.G. Coy. - Company returned to CARENCY by train.	Map LENS 11.
CARENCY	19/11/17		Company marched to BERNEVILLE	
BERNEVILLE	21/11/17		During night of 21/22nd Company marched to COURCELLES-LE-COMTE	Map LENS 11.
COURCELLES LE-COMTE	23/11/17		Company marched to ACHIET-LE-GRAND and entrained and proceeded to FINS - detrained and marched to HEUDICOURT	
HEUDICOURT	24/11/17		Strength decrease during week ending 24/11/17 Nil increase " " " " 24/11/17 1	Map VALENCIENNES 57 572.
	25/11/17		} Sectional training	
	26/11/17			

Army Form C. 2118.

WAR DIARY
or
INTELLIGENCE SUMMARY.
(Erase heading not required.)

Place	Date	Hour	Summary of Events and Information	Remarks and references to Appendices
HEUDICOURT	27/11/17		Company marched to RIBECOURT	
RIBECOURT	28/11/17		night of 28/29th company relieved 2nd & 4th Guards Machine Gun Companies in the FONTAINE – NOTRE – DAME Sector (map 57C. reference F.20.)	
	29/11/17		2ND LT. H.M. DAY returned to company from Transport Course at ABBEVILLE	

FONTAINE – NOTRE – DAME SECTOR	30/11/17		Captain A.J. STEWART returned from leave to U.K. Casualties. 2 O.R. Killed. 5 O.R. wounded. Strength of Company
			
			Officers OR
			10 195
			           30 attched
			           225	

In the field 30/11/17

J Brocklehurst
O/c/dy 174 M.G. Coy.

Army Form C. 2118.

WAR DIARY
or
INTELLIGENCE SUMMARY.
(Erase heading not required.)

Instructions regarding War Diaries and Intelligence Summaries are contained in F. S. Regs., Part II. and the Staff Manual respectively. Title pages will be prepared in manuscript.

Place	Date	Hour	Summary of Events and Information	Remarks and references to Appendices

Vol II

Original

War Diary

of

17th to Machine Gun Company

From 1st Dec 1917

To 31st Dec 1917

Confidential

Army Form C. 2118.

WAR DIARY
or
INTELLIGENCE SUMMARY.
(Erase heading not required.)

174 M.G. Coy.   December 1917

Place	Date	Hour	Summary of Events and Information	Remarks and references to Appendices
FONTAINE/ NOTRE DAME SECTOR	1/12/17		Heavy enemy Barrage. H.E. Gas & Smoke. Casualties 6. O.R. Our 39 Machine Guns fired on movement in LA FONTAINE, + LA FOLIE WOOD & section west & light Boche machine Gun shown one E.A. Aeroplanes hostile and 1+2 M.G. fg. to cover our left flank BOURLON WOOD shelled throughout day	Shear 57c
	2.			
	3.12.17	2.30 p.m	Our S.O.S. sent up, answered by our Artillery. BOURLON WOOD heavily shelled from 4.30 p.m to 5.30 p.m Machine Guns fired on movement in FONTAINE et 4 h nm + throughout day et every enemy from FONTAINE to BOURLON WOOD. 174 M.G. Cy returned by 200 M.G.Cy. Company proceeded to HAVRINCOURT WOOD 2/Lt DODD to Hospital	57c P.19
	4.12.17		Night of 4/5 Company proceeded to METZ EN COUTURE	
	5.12.17		Company proceeded to LECHELLE (P 25 c)	
	6.12.17 to 9.12.17		Interior Economy & sectional training	

Army Form C. 2118.

WAR DIARY
or
INTELLIGENCE SUMMARY.
(Erase heading not required.)

Instructions regarding War Diaries and Intelligence Summaries are contained in F. S. Regs., Part II. and the Staff Manual respectively. Title pages will be prepared in manuscript.

Place	Date	Hour	Summary of Events and Information	Remarks and references to Appendices
LECHELLE	8/12/17		Strength decrease week ending 8.12.17.	SHEET 57c
			2/Lt DODD (wounded Gas)	
			15 O.R (3 wounded 1 missing 9 transferred to 2nd M.G.Coy. 1 transferred to 177 M.G.C.	
			1 to UK (for 6 months)	
FLESQUIERES	10.12.17		Company relieved 2nd M.G.Coy in the line at FLESQUIERES	
	11.12.17		2000 rounds fired harassing Enemy's communications nightly 10/11	
	12.12.17		No day targets. Bad visibility. 9000 rounds fired during night 11/12	
	13.12.17		E. working party at K.12.a.90.60 dispersed by M.G. fire. 6300 rounds fired during night 12/13	
	14.12.17		Working party coming from K.12.a.35.70 dispersed by M.G. fire	
			12,100 rounds harassing fire during night 13/14	
			2/Lt NEVILLE gazetted	
	15.12.17		20,250 rounds fired in sweeping E. area. its keep in a raid planned on E. outpost.	
			Strength increase in strength week ending 15.12.17 O.R 2 Attached O.R. 2	
			Decrease -	O.R 20

Army Form C. 2118.

WAR DIARY
or
INTELLIGENCE SUMMARY.
(Erase heading not required.)

Instructions regarding War Diaries and Intelligence Summaries are contained in F. S. Regs., Part II. and the Staff Manual respectively. Title pages will be prepared in manuscript.

Place	Date	Hour	Summary of Events and Information	Remarks and references to Appendices
FLESQUIERES	15.12.17		Decrease of O.R. 20 caused by Evacuations owing to the effects of Gas in BOURLON WOOD.	Sheet 57 c
	16.12.17		Targets engaged at K.12.a central, 9,500 rounds harassing fire during night 15/16. 2/m M.G. Coy. on completion of relief Company proceeded to RUYAULCOURT. H.Q. P.10.a.7.0 Anti aircraft guns mounted in following positions. 2 at P.32.b.9.3 2 at P.20.c.2.8 2 at O.18.d.1.1 2/Lt HARDY to Hospital.	
RUYAULCOURT	17.12.17		Company Interior Economy.	
	18.12.17		Interior Economy + Sectional Training	
	19.12.17 20.12.17		Company moved to BARASTRE. BARASTRE bombed by E. aircraft	
	21.12.17		Increase in strength during week ending 22.12.17 21 O.R.	
	22.12.17		Decrease " 1 O.R.	
BARASTRE	23.12.17		Company Training. BARASTRE bombed by E. aircraft.	

WAR DIARY
or
INTELLIGENCE SUMMARY.

Army Form C. 2118.

Place	Date	Hour	Summary of Events and Information	Remarks and references to Appendices
BARASTRE	24.12.17		Company training	
	25.12.17		Company entrained for BERLENCOURT	
	26.12.17	2 a.m.	Company arrived at BERLENCOURT	
	27.12.17		Christmas celebrated by the Company. Dinner & concert for the men at Midday. In the evening dinner for the Sergeants, also the Officers.	
	28.12.17		Company training	
	29.12.17		Increase in strength during week ending 29.12.17 NIL O.R. 3	
	30.12.17		Between Church Parades	
	31.12.17		Company training. 2/Lt Tuelite to UK on leave.	

Strength of Company. Officers 10
O.R. 172) 203
Attached 31)

In the field. 31.12.17

T.S. Gibson K.A.4
174 M.G. Co.

Army Form C. 2118.

WAR DIARY
or
INTELLIGENCE SUMMARY.
(Erase heading not required.)

Vol 12 — Continuation

Original

War Diary

of

114th Machine Gun Company

From 1st Jan 1918
to 31st Jan 1918.

Army Form C. 2118.

WAR DIARY
or
INTELLIGENCE SUMMARY.
(Erase heading not required.)

174 M.G. Coy.   January 1918

Place	Date	Hour	Summary of Events and Information	Remarks and references to Appendices
BERLENCOURT	Jan 1		Company training. 2/Lt IREDALE to U.K. on leave	51c 1/40000
	2		Company training. Brigade tactical scheme for H.Q. staff. Rastgrnn LIENCOURT	
			Counter attack on SARS-LEZ-BOIS and MAGNICOURT	
	3		Company Training	
	4		Brigade tactical scheme for all Officers & H.Q. staff. Repetition of scheme of 2.1.18	
	5		Surprise practice move of Company at a moments notice.	
			Increase in strength week ending 5.1.18 1 O.R.	
			Decrease " " " 10 O.R.	
	6		Church Parade	
	7		Company training	
	8		Brigade tactical scheme. Counter attack on LIENEREUIL from LIENCOURT	
	9		Company training. Staff ride for Officers in afternoon 2/Lt McCORMICK reported for duty & taken on strength of Company	
	10		Company training	

Army Form C. 2118.

WAR DIARY
or
INTELLIGENCE SUMMARY.
(Erase heading not required.)

Instructions regarding War Diaries and Intelligence Summaries are contained in F. S. Regs., Part II. and the Staff Manual respectively. Title pages will be prepared in manuscript.

Place	Date	Hour	Summary of Events and Information	Remarks and references to Appendices
BERLENCOURT	11.1.18		Brigade Tactical Exercise. Company defended SARS lez BOIS & retired on MAGNICOURT. 2/5 N Staff + 2/5 S. Staff Battalion attacked from DENIER	51^C 1.40.000
	12		Company Training. Strength increase for week 7 O.R.	
	13		Church Parade. " " Decrease " " 2 O.R.	
	14		Coy Training. Brigade Staff ride. Withdrawing from successive positions between DENIER & BEAUFORT.	
	15		Company at Range. 2/Lt NICOLL to III CORPS INF SCHOOL	
	16		Company Training	
	17		Company Training 2/Lt IREDALE rejoined from leave (U.K.)	
	18		Company Training	
	19		Strength Increase for week 11 O.R. 3 O.R. attached	
	20		Decrease " —	
			Church Parade.	
	21-22		Company Training	
	23		Company at Range I 25. t.	

Army Form C. 2118.

WAR DIARY
or
INTELLIGENCE SUMMARY.
(Erase heading not required.)

Place	Date	Hour	Summary of Events and Information	Remarks and references to Appendices
BERLENCOURT	24 Jan 18		Company training. Staff ride for Officers and Sergeants. Inspection of Box Respirators.	5/1.C /M/3000
	25		Brigade Tactical Scheme. Withdrawing rear covering position. SARS-LEZ-BOIS to BEAUFORT.	
	26		G.O.C's Inspection of Company and transport. 1 O.R. 3/Sgt Wilson E. No 16941 to hospital sick.	
	27		Strength decrease 1 O.R Church Parades.	
	28		Revolver Practice on Range. Company Training. 1st days class of instruction on Lewis Gun commenced for Lewis Gun section. Heavy and light Batt[?] in Brigade. 8 O.R from Batt[?] in Brigade No 21543 Sgt Penny J "Mentioned in Despatches London Gazette 24/11/17.	
	29		Company on Machine Gun Range. Company Training.	
	30		C.O's Parade. Company Training. Brigade Cross Country Race. No 67547 Sgt W Kenny to England for Commission.	
	31		Company training. 170 O.Rs 34 attacked Strength of Company 10 Officers Total 214	B McDary 2/Lt RWF Coy a/adjt 17th RWF Coy

Army Form C. 2118.

WAR DIARY
INTELLIGENCE SUMMARY.
(Erase heading not required.)

Instructions regarding War Diaries and Intelligence Summaries are contained in F. S. Regs., Part II. and the Staff Manual respectively. Title pages will be prepared in manuscript.

Place	Date	Hour	Summary of Events and Information	Remarks and references to Appendices

Vol 13

Confidential

Original War Diary
of
174th Machine Gun Company

From :- 1st Feby 1918
To :- 28th Feby 1918

WAR DIARY or INTELLIGENCE SUMMARY

Army Form C. 2118.

Place	Date	Hour	Summary of Events and Information	Remarks and references to Appendices
BERLENCOURT	1.2.18		174 M.G Coy February 1918	51 c 1:40000
			Company training. Brigade Tactical scheme for H.Q Staff	
	2.		Strength week ending 2.2.18 3 O.R (attached)	
			" " 19 O.R 6 O.R (attached)	
	3.		Church Parades	
	4.		Brigade Route March	
	5.		Inspection by Corps Commander	
	6.		Company training	
	7.		Company training	
	8.		Company left billets at BERLENCOURT and marched to BIENVILLERS and remained there for one night 8th-9th. Lt Kitchener and 6 O.R formed the advance party and reported to 120th M.G Coy in the evening the night sector the 40th Divisional front to obtain information for the relief. Lt Greaves & and 1 O.R formed the billeting party for the company at BIENVILLERS	

Army Form C. 2118.

WAR DIARY
or
INTELLIGENCE SUMMARY.
(Erase heading not required.)

Instructions regarding War Diaries and Intelligence Summaries are contained in F. S. Regs, Part II. and the Staff Manual respectively. Title pages will be prepared in manuscript.

Place	Date	Hour	Summary of Events and Information	Remarks and references to Appendices
BIENVILLERS	9/5/18.		Company left BIENVILLERS at 7.30am and proceeded to DURROW Camp MORY to relieve 102 M.G. Coy in 40th Divisional Reserve. The section officers went ahead to reconnoitre Rear position to be taken up in case of alarm. On arrival at DURROW CAMP at 12 midday the company was under orders with limber packed and guns ready to move at short notice to positions reconnoitred by Section Officers 2/PH NEWTON'S true to U.K. Strength for week ending 9/5/18 - 10.O.R. 2 alt.	
DURROW CAMP MORY.	10/5/18.		Church Parades. Capt. Stewart Lt. BRACKENRIDGE, IRELAND & Lt. SILVERMAN, 6.O.R. reported Company.	2.O.R. 1 alt.
	11/5/18.		Company relieved the 120 M.G. Coy in the RIGHT SECTOR (NOREUIL). Relief Complete 9.20 p.m. 10.R. wounded.	
NOREUIL E of BULLECOURT	12/5/18.		Transport Lines - Q.M. Stores moved to DESART CAMP 9000 rounds fired on selected targets by guns in PAKWAY RESERVE night of 12/5 & 13.	
	13/5/18.		Lt. SILVERMAN, 1.O.R. proceeded to CAMIERS to attend No. 52 M.G. Course. Sniping guns put in positions in a field 500 yds at Enemy Parties. 9000 fired on H.Q. and tracks throughout night.	
	14/5/18.		D.M.G.O. went round all guns. Exceedingly quiet day. 8500 useful shots projection and heavy shelling of front line by the enemy throughout night. 1.O.R. bombed 1.O.R. wounded (gas)	

A7092. Wt. W125 9/16/1393. 75000. 1/17. D. D. & L. Ltd. Forms/C2118/44.

Army Form C. 2118.

WAR DIARY
or
INTELLIGENCE SUMMARY.
(Erase heading not required.)

Instructions regarding War Diaries and Intelligence
Summaries are contained in F. S. Regs., Part II.
and the Staff Manual respectively. Title pages
will be prepared in manuscript.

Place	Date	Hour	Summary of Events and Information	Remarks and references to Appendices
	15/2/18.		Very quiet. Rifle and M.G. fire at night. 3000 rounds fired on tracks and movement by enemy during night. Put up our S.O.S. lines at 10 p.m.	
	16/2/18.		More activity during the day. Both artillery and aeroplanes. After self-relief took place. 5,000 rounds night. Strong SOS sent up for short enemy M.G. 4 O.R. 17 O.R. decrease	
	17/2/18.		Sniping. Guns fired 1500 rounds on enemy movements during the day. Fired at night on enemy communications. Two guns from that line moved to DEWDROP TRENCH	
	18/2/18.		Movement near RIENCOURT appreciably lessened by sniping guns during the day. Harassing fire carried out at night.	
	19/2/18.		Quiet day. Usual harassing fire carried out at night.	
	20/2/18.		Extremely quiet. Harassing fire at enemy Co. 2/Lt W Breckenridge went back to Transport Lines to proceed on leave to UK.	
	21/2/18.		Held section relief took place during the afternoon. 2/5 N&S Regt. regarded back from III Corps Inf. School and proceeded to RAILWAY RESERVE Group. Harassing fire was carried out at night and some movement engaged during the day.	
	22/3/18.		Quiet. Harassing fire at night carried out.	
	23/3/18.		Enemy artillery was active during the day. 2/Lt Breckenridge and 2 O.R. G.S.K leave. He usual harassing fire was carried out by us during the night. Strength average for week ending 23rd 10ff. 13 O.R. 7 S.R. attd. 30 O.R. 1 O.R. attd. decrease	

WAR DIARY or INTELLIGENCE SUMMARY

Army Form C. 2118.

Place	Date	Hour	Summary of Events and Information	Remarks and references to Appendices
	24/5/18		Fairly quiet. More hostile aerial activity. 1500 rounds fired of F.A. used harassing fire at night.	
	25/5/18		More activity on the part of enemy artillery during the day. Harassing fire carried on at night. Capt Shaw attended conference at H.Q. Staffords and Company Commanders of new battalion Co Balk. 2/Lt Heston proceeded on leave to U.K. 2/Lt McCormick to hospital sick. Relief change of officers.	
	26/5/18		Quiet day. Relief carried out during the forenoon. Usual number of rounds fired in enemy communication ways away to the night. 2/Lt P.H. Heston returned home leave to U.K.	
	27/5/18		Quiet during morning and night. County Battery work during the afternoon. RAILWAY RESERVE Guns fired 1500 rounds at enemy trails. Headquarters during the night. 2/Lt Fisher and 18 O.R. joined for duty.	
	28/5/18		Quiet day except for concentration on NORFUL VALLEY during the afternoon. The usual harassing fire was carried out during the night.	
			Strength of Company 12 Officers 180 O.R.	1 Officer & attached 26 O.R.

Joseph McDay Lt
17th M.S. Con

www.ingramcontent.com/pod-product-compliance
Lightning Source LLC
Chambersburg PA
CBHW081432160426
43193CB00013B/2260